Keepin' It Real, Always

Always

inside the mind of Elite

Jeffrey DeLaRosa

authorHOUSE®

AuthorHouse™
1663 Liberty Drive
Bloomington, IN 47403
www.authorhouse.com
Phone: 1-800-839-8640

Published by AuthorHouse 2/7/2012

ISBN: 978-1-4670-9797-0 (sc)
ISBN: 978-1-4670-9796-3 (hc)
ISBN: 978-1-4670-9795-6 (e)

Library of Congress Control Number: 2011960398

Printed in the United States of America

This book is dedicated to those who love poetry,
To those who I love, and to those who love me.
Keep it real, always.

DISCLAIMER

BEWARE!

Proceed with extreme caution.

This is a direct and clear warning to approach this book and all of its content with an open mind and an open heart. Never draw conclusions, but by all means feel free to make your own interpretations.

The material in this bound collection of pages contains work of actual accounts 100% accurate and positively genuine feelings, memories, dedications, stories, and depictions of actual places, people, things, emotions, and events all written using nothing but pure, deep, unpredictable, unadulterated, and unprecedented honesty.

Like a preemptive assault on your character and your person, it incorporates often controversial reality, truth, passion, experience and most importantly love.

The information therein includes no fiction beyond that fabricated by the neither conscious nor subconscious mind. It attacks the inner soul in a unique yet effective manner. Sometimes explicit and graphic in nature, but never with the intent to neither harm nor offend. Readers' discretion is strongly advised.

CONTENTS

CHAPTER 5 — GUILLOTINE

CHAPTER 6 — LOVE AND ROMANCE

CHAPTER 7 — DARKNESS

CHAPTER 8 — EPILOGUE

INTRODUCTION

PROLOGUE

Door opens up
I walk thru stuck up
But head down
The opening scene is now seen
Now I'm senile
Prestige personified
Maliciously clean
Introductory credits unfold
Slowly I turn
Exposed
Watching over my shoulder cautiously
Isn't enough
In singulars and plurals
Refined and yet far from rural
My minds unfurled
The gates close shut
Welcome to my world!

-ELITE-

KEEPIN IT REAL, ALWAYS

WRITER'S PROFILE

Name: Jeffrey Jayce De La Rosa

Born: November 6th, 1983

Birthplace: Passaic, New Jersey USA

Hair: Black

Eyes: Brown

Height: 6'1

Weight: 180 LBS

Nationality: Latino/Dominican

Favorite Color: Blue

Favorite Number: One

Favorite Sports Teams: New York Yankees, New York Knicks, and New York Giants

Favorite Sports Figures: Derek Jeter, Allan Houston

Favorite Movies: Rocky 1-6, Independence Day

Favorite Music: Hip Hop, Rhythm and Blues, Merengue, Bachata, and Pop

Favorite Book: The Alchemist by Paulo Coelho

Hobbies: Reading, Writing, Tennis, Basketball, Billiards, Dominos

Moto: Keep it real, always, be you at all cost

Alter Ego/Alias: Elite

Favorite Poet: Black Ice, Maya Angelou

Passion: Poetry

Writing styles: Rhyme, Lyric, Analogy, Blank Verse, Conceit, Free Verse, Romanticism, Carpe Diem, with a hip hop flavor.

Who is Elite

OFFICIAL DEFINITION OF ELITE

1. Privileged minority
A small group of people within a larger group who have more power, social standing, wealth, or talent than the rest of the group.

2. Richest, best, or most powerful
More talented, privileged, or highly trained than others.

MY DEFINITION:

Who and what "Elite" means and is to me differs from the dictionary's meaning. In a way it does represent being and/or wanting to be the best at something. Coming from nothing and trying to excel at something in this case that strive would be writing/poetry. When I say I am elite, I am by no stretch of the imagination saying I am better then anyone. Elite is the moniker that keeps me humble and sane.

"Elite" is that persona, that character if you will, that other side of me that everybody has who is the total opposite of the person that often stands out. "Elite" brings out the inner genius in me. He brings out the cockiness and the un precedented confidence in me. He is the one who speaks for me in times when I cannot find the words or when I am hesitant to speak out openly. He allows me to express myself in a manner that shows no remorse, no apologies, and most importantly of all, no lies.

Without "Elite" this book would not be possible. "Elite" is the hood in me. It is the ghetto in me. It signifies the struggle, the hustle, and represents the life and times of the mind of a poet. He created the slogan "keeping it real, always" to remind us to be yourself at all times, at any expense, and by all means necessary.

Elite is not who I want to be but who I have to be.

He writes in ways that I cannot. He speaks in ways that demand attention. He expresses himself in ways that is often questioned. He is the anti-hero to the hero inside me. He is simply a vigilante. "Elite" is the street that makes the words visually come alive out of the page.

Quite frankly without him I wouldn't have the swagger that makes me who I am

K.I.R.A

ELITE

Apocalypse is coming take hold of your weapon
Mines a pen the end is near see me in heaven
Revolutionary thoughts when I react on a sheet
Unravel your mind when I teach
Very fluent when I speak
Educate your mind when I'm describing the streets
Analyzing the heat
Bringing peace never beef
Reality stands for everything that I mean
When I bring havoc unleashed
I release fire at least
At best, I'm stone cold bringing chills to your chest
I spit serendipity
Verses of doom laid out on the piece
True knowledge exposed when I speak out I'm elite!

7/08

ELITE ACROSTIC

Keen are the words, as they inhabit the earth

Earthly is elite overcoming the hurt

Elite is prestige always finishing first

Prestige is intellect acquired at birth

Intellect is naturally obtained after putting in work

Natural is the ghetto flow keeping it raw

Ghetto is the mind set humbling your intuition with war

Intuitive tame instincts are a powerful flaw

Tamed beasts never forget what their really hear for

Real is elegance when you absolutely don't accept false

Elegant is the mass appeal that attracts who you are

Appeal is legitimately necessary

Legit is no counterfeit but on the contrary you have to

ALWAYS! Leave your mark inevitably

-ELITE-

Elite's random thoughts

Elite is the poet within me
He takes something calm and turns it into a frenzy
He takes something vague
And makes it clear as day
He can take any word and transform it into an art form
With metaphors
Turns a phrase into a masterpiece
Turns every page into his master sheet
Like a slave obeying when the master speaks
Thru all the phases of his life you read
He helps maintain my sanity
He's the eye in me
My alter ego
My alias, my being
Elites the hand behind the pen
The vision, the eyes, the mind behind the lens
I have no control over what he writes
All I know is that when he's done
My pen shines bright
I suddenly take over like a vigilante
Infiltrate your style
And sabotage your paper
I take creative control
Action
No authorization granted
Vision slanted
The plane has landed
As I creep thru like a masked bandit
I am stamped branded
It's real

-ELITE-

POETRY

DEFINITION AND STRUCTURE

Definition of Poetry
Poetry is a piece of literature written by a poet in meter or verse expressing various emotions, which are expressed by the use of variety of techniques including metaphors, similes and onomatopoeia. The emphasis on the aesthetics of language and the use of techniques such as repetition, meter, and rhyme are what are commonly used to distinguish poetry from prose. Poems often make heavy use of imagery and word association to quickly convey emotions.

Structure of Poetry
The structure used in poems varies with different types of poetry. The structural elements include the line, couplet, strophe and stanza. Poets combine the use of language and a specific structure to create imaginative and expressive work. The structure used in some Poetry types is also used when considering the visual effect of a finished poem. The structure of many types of poetry results in groups of lines on the page which enhance the poem's composition.

LOVE OF MY LIFE

I met her in high school
I found her cool
She made me feel a certain way
That nobody could
So deep, original, unique, and so sweet
At times I would just sit back and listen to her speak
Type of chick you could vibe with
Rhyme with, smile with, even cry with
She was popular, but many dudes were afraid to be seen with her
Even if they messed with her, they often kept it to themselves for sure
I didn't care I showed her off
I showed that I was soft
She made me more attractive to girls
At least so I thought
I was faithful as I did her all thru high school
And then relaxed
Later on, I realized I wanted her back
She was a pastime, a hobby that I used when I was bored
And as I grew older, I needed her more
Therefore, it went from a fling to actually going steady
She was my main squeeze although she had been already
She was into my flow, my swag,
And the way I could write
In her name, I could bless a paper onsite
With only a pen we survived and became closer and tighter
I would write poems about her
I was inspired
She made me brighter
She was my provider
But mentally
She would stimulate me emotionally and spiritually
Never physically
Our relationship wasn't physical
She is my passion and I mean it literal
She is what drives me and I mean in general

With her I can clown around
I've analyzed and studied her up and down
I get excited every time when she comes around
Commercial and underground
She's been profound since the ultrasound
She's everything to me she's my environment
She has met everybody except my parents
And she understands
Her and I will die together pen and page in hand
She's my best friend
The one I go to when I need to vent
She'll always comfort me during times of stress
She opens up to many people but I have love and respect
For she's the only one that can fuck with my head
My feelings evolved
I went from loving her to being in love
With only her words, she can *gimme* a hug
I do her out of passion; I do her for the love
Some do her for the money, others just because
She does it free
She's a slut but she's clean
I come to her when the skies are gray
In fact, I don't think I would be able to make it thru the day

She completes me in every way
I go to her night morning or day
I can talk to her about my past, my present, my future
I've told her all and she understood,
No matter the topic it's always all good
When she spreads her legs, I spread my wings
She puts my right hand to work as I begin to think
Serene
Even if we break up she'll always be apart of me
Thru my history, she is my destiny
My whole ecstasy
My only reason for being
My liberty
Forever the love of my life
Poetry

-ELITE-

5-15-09

ESSENCE OF POETRY

In my world, poetry is of the essence. It is of the greatest importance, crucial, somewhat like time... priceless and timeless like wine. By nature, essentially my mind labors in poetic fashion causing poetic justice.
It exists, it incorporates everything I stand and live by and for... The essence being the most important ingredient, in poetry that would be honesty, the humility you bring to express yourself in a zone caring less about your surroundings as u interpret justice onto a page, and keeping it real is of the poetic essence in the ELITE realm of thinking..
As I find myself traveling solo most of the time in this poetically determined conquest, to get my messages across, I see that I do not lead a path alone, for I have steps that carry on beside me. They being of my P.P.I.C (poetic partner in crime), your title became my thoughts.
My thoughts became an art
This art form we share is of high significance, but only because to our souls, it is of "THE ESSENCE"
Your passion for equality, your understanding for a love that which I share, is perhaps irreplaceable...
As your dome swells like a helium-filled balloon, I smile, knowing I have put a smile on your face bringing nothing but honesty, humility, and artisanship in my way. All being my elements of the essence of poetry...
There are only five elements of evil: Lust, Envy, Jealousy, Greed, and Hate... and as long as I have the three elements of poetry: Honesty, Humility, and Passion, I will nevermore submit to evil!
As I conclude historically,
just know that right now you are the essence of my poetry
-ELITE-

5/06

15

MY POETRY

Poetry is a gift, it is piff when I spit.
Knowing what you get, every time is the shit
darkness turns bright; every night when I write
my mind becomes loose when my rhymes become tight
It sets me free, as I escape the world's miseries
when the world rejects, poetry lets me be.
It lets my body relax makes happiness begin
I will continue this art form until the day of the end.
When all the doors close, a poem lets me in
Into a completely new world with all friends no foes, some
jokes no hoes, but in concentration mode, as long as there is a
pen I will never be alone!
It gets my mind going, my blood starts flowing, my feelings
start showing, my heart starts glowing, and I get excited like a
little kid when it starts snowing...
It is unexplainable, understandable but separates me from the
rest, so I guess its seperational!
It is a passion, my poetry's in action; it allows me to express
myself in artistic fashion.
Until I settle down poetry is my wifey, but forever in a days,
poetry is my life bee
Tuesday, May 02, 2006
-ELITE-

SUMMER HAIKU

Different colors

Now appearing before us

As heat takes over the land

WHEN I WRITE

When I write it is lopsided
One sided affair when my pen and page are united
Collided
Poetry with a nasty flow
Crazy loco hunchback Quasimodo
Hydro smoke blow
Natural high that rise up to your nose bone
Stone cold smoking skull
From a world, that has me in a chokehold
Strangled I fold like a bad hand
Embrace the cards I'm dealt
My feelings are heart felt
Emotional tremendous but subliminally
Horrendous
Never visual
Nothing physically is visibly noticeable
Nomad
But interiorly
Enough energy to part seas
I never wish hurt on no man
That's my word man
But I kill'em on a sheet
As I watch the crime rate increase
Murder rates ridiculously obscene
Unseen
Unity is a state of mind when you're clean
Ask the queen
Me not writing is like waking up from a good dream

-ELITE-

7/08

DECODING THE PAST

SUPERBOWL SUNDAY

This has nothing to do with football, but everything to do with escaping reality. It does not rhyme and it may be corny even cheesy. However, it is what it is and they are my feelings now in time. Loneliness, at a time when I should be here watching the game with you instead of writing this. I mean I am still watching the game, but its halftime right now and Paul McCartney is singing some bullshit, which is just depressing me more. How old do they think the people watching this are?

I do not eat in the morning thinking about you. I do not eat in the evening thinking about you. At night, I cannot sleep because I am hungry! I am being somewhat humorous in order to mask the pain. Laughter is necessary through tough times in life. I actually do eat. Too much sometimes, but my fast metabolism prevents it from showing. Kudos to my metabolic and digestive system.

I try hard not to miss you. I tell myself I do not. I am in denial. I am afraid. I am sad. I am alone!

Do I miss your touch? Your smile? Your scent? Your ass? Your presence? Your overall company or am I kidding myself? Perhaps I just miss having someone. Someone to fill the huge gap, which is the void that you have left. The more I try to forget about you the more I think about you. The more I hate you for not sticking with me the more I miss you. It is not fare. Maybe if I would have cheated on you, hit you, lied to you, maybe you would have wanted me in your life. For the ones that give 110% in a relationship, honest, give their all, are the ones given up on. Ain't that a bitch.

Do not dare say you loved me as much as I loved you. That will never be true. Long shot. Not in a million years. It was never equal. You were the first to know everything while I was always last. You were always my first, sometimes too often, while I was often second or 3rd.

As the patriots and the eagles kill themselves in this 7-7 tie, my emotions are killing me. Wait…TOUCHDOWN! New England just took a 14-7 lead. Like my feelings, they vary from hour to hour. I want you but I do not. I want you and I do not. I need you, but I guess I really do not. I am still here! I do not care about this game, except that

I have money on the pats. I do not care if there is food even though I must eat. Do not care if there is air even though I must breath. Do not matter if there is any gas because my car no longer has anywhere to go. I guess I am old fashioned, but I like happy endings. I guess there is none here except for the fact that I have sports to distract my mind from you momentarily.

Just wished you would have loved me the same way that I loved you. As I keep pouring my mind, heart, and soul on paper, eventually I will move on and life will be good again.

Oh, shit! Show me the money!

The patriots won! 24-21!

Fuck you pay me!

-ELITE-

2-6-05

LYRICAL SUICIDE

Visions of nightmares dancing through my head
Apocalypse is near I'm alive but I'm dead.
I'm present in the future but the past is seen red.
Blood flows Armageddon's further then first said.
Too close to stay calm or turn back run forward instead.
As the earth rotates
Everyone has likes and distastes
All flavors have to be tasted
Regardless if it's sweet, sour, our grape
Life's great if you learn to learn from mistakes
When you don't grasp it becomes a disgrace
My words are like a million man march
Follow or chase
I inspire through the wire with no affiliation to known society
or race
Faith
I have my own beliefs and my own mentality
My own grief and my own harsh realities
My own Christianity
My own insanity
Originality
At the same time genuine superficiality
Artificiality has overtaken this planet
Dammit
I quit
Cause quite frankly I've had it!

-ELITE-

Revised from 1-5-05

HIP-HOP

NO BEEF/SLICK LYRICS ON A HOT BEAT/ITS ALL
PEACE/ BEAT BOXIN BODY POPPIN,LOCKIN,SWIFT
MOVES UNIQUE SENSE OF STYLE/ABILITY
TO WILD OUT/ TRENDY FASHIONS,DURAGS,
FITTEDS, DOWN TO THE TIMBOOTS/COMES
NATURALLY FROM YOUR ROOTS/
THE WALK THE TALK ITS ALL YOU
UNWRITTEN RULES, DRESS CODES THE LAWS
OF THE JUNGLE THE STREETS HOME/R N B
FLOWS/ COMIN UP FROM THE GUTTER/MAKIN
THE BUTTER, WALLS COVERED IN GRAFFITTI/
POPPIN WU-TANG IN THE CD/BUMPIN IN YOUR
WHIP CRUISIN/ WHILE YOU FREE YA MIND IS
SOOTHING/ CERTAIN MIND STATE/OUTSIDE
GROUPS CAN'T RELATE/BEFORE YOU SNITCH
YOU GOTTA PLEAD THE FIFTH/ THIS SHITS
LEGIT, TIGHT METAPHORS/ ALWAYS KEEPIN
IT RAW/ THE RHYTHM,IT'S A STATE OF MIND/
AGELESS LIKE TIME/IT'S A WAY OF LIFE/ LIKE ME
SAYIN POETRYS MY WIFE/A RARE COMPARISON
DESPITE/THE FACT I FEEL IM DESCRIBING THIS
RIGHT/
IT'S ALL FAIR, BLOW YA WEED SMOKE IN THE
AIR/ IM DOING THIS PAPER JUSTICE/EXPLAINING
THIS IS OUR LIFE TRUST THIS/ CONTAINING
MANY LEVELS, SOME FORMENTIONED, DJ-ING,
MC-ING, POETRY'S DIVIDED INTO SECTIONS/ WE

CAN ALL RELATE, WORLDWIDE CONNECTIONS/
IT CRYS FOR COLLABORATIONS/ IN THIS GAME
WE ALL FAMILY/LISTEN TO A TUNE HELPS US
THROUGH TRAGEDIES/
DANCIN,DANCEFLOOR PACKED/FREESTYLE IN
THE CYPHER WIT KATS, PITTEN A RAP/POETRYS
BORN.YOU EITHER HAVE IT OR YOU DON'T BUT
STILL DONT TRY TO IGNORE
WHETHER YOU KNOW WHAT IT IS YOU CAN
FEEL IT IN MY PRESENCE/ITS VIRTUALLY OF
THE ESSENCE/FULLA ENTERTAINMENT AND
AN OCCASIONAL LESSON/but always with a message/
IT SPONSORS THE SCHOOL OF HARD KNOCKS/
ITS ALL OVER YA HOOD IN EVERY BLOCK/EVERY
SPOT/CREATOR OF SLANG DESIGNER GEAR THAT
SHIT HOT/THINK IT,WRITE IT DOWN, LIVE IT
DON'T EVER STOP/
IF YOUR FAKE QUIT IT/SPIT IT/OUT, HIT IT/
BUT STRAP IT/UP, MY PEN AINT SHOT/ FEEL
THE SHOCK/THINK, THEN STOP/IT'S IN YOUR
EVERYDAY VOCABULARY, IT'S MY LOVE, ITS HIP
HOP!/
11/04/06
-ELITE-

INTERNAL JOURNEY

Intellectual thoughts traveling through the minds inner design
are those I absorb through the blind
Observe the times. A battles been fought combat through
a war, collide with your thoughts analyze what you brought
to the table, no need for remorse Ideas circulate randomly
penetrate occasionally actions quicker than reactions, they
hesitate. I'm direct verbally no misconceptions, concepts make
the globe rotate, but at your own pace as long as you get there,
you're never late. I isolate on this heat, regulate on a sheet, so
that strait out my dome you can sample a peace
ordinarily not shallow, but on the thick chick love the booty
that's not narrow I'm talking one that's too much for me to
swallow or handle but that isn't all but it's a hassle
Internally, now days these broads are a gamble, originality
and humility are stressed by example. Lead by a series of acts
there is no lead in this pen, 2gether we task just read on, but
moments in life at a time and there should be no questions to
ask
I am launching a global warning somewhat like Al Gores 10
year advanced warning of global warming
apocalypse arrives all we have is accomplishments Armageddon
fails, you take with you acknowledgements my compliments
go to those that are positive but true, I take to my grave beliefs
and self theories, enough in the brain to publish a bible of my
own feelings my point of views aren't altered by any known
force but mine I decide, in my chamber, who rules. Bluntly, I
can be warm or cold, but GOD and the devil both have dibs on
this soul
6/22/06

-Elite-

COMFORT ZONE

On the court I'm balling
Three points falling
H to the izzo phenomenon
Waters pouring
It rains
Its all day
That's the killer Jay
Murdering the opposition
No competition
You're reaching while I'm teaching
Just watch and listen
As the swish burns the net
You feel the heat in your neck
From the ammunition
Fingertips in the air
Wrist cracking
It's on a mission
No intermission
As long as I'm in a win win position
Its skill not superstition
For real, it's an addiction
The clutch is always in good conditions
Intuitions
Shots draining
I'm maintaining as long as I'm winning
I'm not complaining
I'm in my war zone

-ELITE-

Revised from 7/05

ANOTHER UNTITLED

The devil attempts to tempt me
He often succeeds
As I fail to break free
Therefore, I stare at the mirror and smile
Knowing that tomorrow the sun will come out
I go thru metamorphosis on a daily basis
Waiting for the day where Armageddon sets in
Most times, I'm stressing
Don't wanna die, but sometimes
It feels like death is endless
Unlike life
When I write my mental styles tremendous
My sorrows clever
Eternal life
Cause when I die my writings last forever
I'm like a knight and the pen is my sword
With might I sever with force
The heads of those who do not cherish the thoughts
Of course, I go straight to the source
Not looking back but going forward I'm lost
In this land with no remorse
Going hard
I wake up from a bad dream
But the devil is still at large

-ELITE-

2008

JUST A THOUGHT

No man fails you either quit or u die
know that the journey continues as long as your alive
the struggles go on, wipe your tears after u cry/ but get up and
fight, don't die
I never lie/true ill will the drive/ is modest and humble the
mega vibe/ is that I bring when I collide/ on a sheet, triumph,
victory on a rhyme/ as I succeed through your mind/ thoughts
travel in apocalyptic size/ mega hawk as I analyze the peace of
the pie/don't hate, that be the fake Jake niggas who trapped in
they own gates/ my punctualities never late/ my brain never my
thoughts it confiscates/
this is real talk from my own thoughts/ never copy cat fuck
what u heard my shit isn't bought/ its authentically crafted,
verbal foul and drastic/but classic/sensitive crazy whatever but
forever lasting/
your given the playing field now play the game/play the cards
that your dealt the rest is to remain/a few muscles you'll strain/
never point a finger your the only one to blame/you control
your own destiny with help but your own brain/I control my
own fame/ I rather keep it real then suffer internal pains/
real is how I like to keep it always, you know the drill/ do the
same, u cool wit me, u know the dill/ this rhyme wasn't written
it was typed strait out the grill/ fresh out the dome peace hot
just like my mills/
if I don't receive your props after this rhyme I'll have to take it/
but everything I say is mine, u can't make or brake it/
I'm unique in every sense/ fuck the beef lets make amends/ I'm
a menace when I spit words that seek revenge/ its like putting
words 2gether was given to me as a 6th sense/I carry on precise
and intense/ but also, flip it nice real light wit no expense/

I say I'm different in every way shape or form/but really we all the same except the race shape and form/ I lace and grace this platform/ wit simple metaphors that make your mind far from norm/
look me in the eyes and instantly you'll get caught/ havoc's unleashed as you learned u was taught/ just know to be yourself is the lesson I brought/ until u find your way you will forever be lost/ have your own theories, styles, and beliefs at any cost/no matter who u work for forever u remain your own boss/however u see fit but don't judge me as soft/ I'm interchangeable a lyrical war has just been fought/ victorious I stand within myself, this just a thought!!
-ELITE-
5/08/06

MEMORIES LAST

DIRTY MAGAZINES BEING A FEEN WERE PARTS
OF GROWING UP AS A TEEN. NOT CHASING THE
GREEN. SLEEP WITH NO DREAMS. IN A SOCIETY
THAT IS NOT ON YOUR TEAM.

PEOPLE DISSIN TAP KISSIN HEARIN BUT NEVER
LISTEN
SCHOOL CRUSHES, STUPID MISTAKES ERASE
THE HATE ON THESE FOOLS, TOUCH'EM.

TIME ESCAPES, HORSEPLAYIN, CUTTIN CLASS
IS NOW A THING OF THE PAST CAN'T DITCH
LIFE I DISH OUT WORDS TO EXPLAIN WHEN
TIMES WERE RIGHT YA FIRST NIGHT, YA FIRST
LIGHT FIRST TIME YA DID SOMETHING TRIFE IS
DISTANT MEMORIES OF YOUR TEEN LIFE WHEN
WAS THE LAST TIME YOU DID SOMETHING
NICE?

REMEMBER YOUR FIRST TIME BEING PULLED
OVER BY COPS? REMEMBER BEING PULLED OUT
FROM INSIDE THE WOUND? PROBLY NOT
IM SURE YOU REMEMBER GRADUATING FROM
SCHOOL, OR THE FIRST WHOOPING YOU GOT.

AS TIMES GO BY YOU REMINISCE ABOUT THE
PLEASUREABLE THINGS VIRGINITY LOST
ITEMS WERE BOUGHT LIKE DIAMONDS AND
RINGS MATERIAL THINGS ARENT WHATS
VALUABLE.

MOST IMPORTANTLY THE MEMORIES THAT
YOU KEEP ALLOW YOU TO RELIVE THEM IN THE
PRESENT AS YOU SPEAK

THE TASTES AND SOUNDS OF A YOUNG
PAST, KEEP YOU PERMANENTLY NAIVE IN AN
INNOCENT AND ADULT FUTURE. AS STRUGGLES
COME AND PASS WE ARE APPROACHING OUR
LAST,
DAYS THINK ABOUT AND CHERISH THE BEST
ONES IT GETS WORSE TIME MACHINE? YOU
WONT GET ONE; LIVE THE CURSE TO ITS
FULLEST.

THINKIN BACK LETS YOU LIVE FOREVER IN
PEACE. SUMMERTIME, GETTIN HOME DRINKIN
SHOP-RITE ICE TEA.

NEVER TOOK FOR GRANTED THE LESS
FORTUNATE DAYS
STILL HAD EVERYTHING IN THE WORLD
CONSTANTLY STEPPIN ON ROACHES AVOIDING
THE PATH OF A RAT, WHO WERE MORE LIKE
MICE FLIPPIN CHANNELS, A-C ON, FEELIN NICE.

REFRIGERATOR WASNT FULL BUT NEVER
EMPTY. DAD SAID I HAD IT GOOD PERHAPS I
STILL DO, WE GET PLENTY CHANCES TO MAKE
THINGS WRONG, NOT MANY TO MAKE IT
RIGHT.
WISH I COULD GO BACK TO THEM DAYS!

PEEWEE HERMAN ON THE TUBE JUMPING OFF
THE COUCH TRYNA FLY, STARING OUT THE
WINDOW AT NITE HOPING TO SEE SANTA HO-
HO HOVERING THROUGH THE SKY.
 MOST OF YOUR CHILDHOOD IS LIES BUT ALL
GROWN UP NOW THE TRUTH MAKES YOU DIE I
RATHER BE ALIVE.

HATE IS WASTED ENERGY, LIVE, LOVE, LIFE BUT
NOTHINGS FOREVER. YOU PASS IT DOWN TO
THE ONES YOU BECOME, THE SEEDS
IT IS AN ETERNAL CYCLE BUT WHERE DOES IT
LEAD?
THEY METAMORPH INTO US, SPITTEN IMAGE
CARBON COPY SOMETIMES YOU GET THE
FEELING OF DEJAVU. AINT IT SOMETHIN?

YOU LOOK AT YOUR FUTURE AND YOUR PAST
AND LAUGH BUT HONESTLY, MEMORIES ARE
THE ONLY THING IN THIS WORLD THAT LAST!

 -ELITE-

SILENT KILLER

Momentary silence when I spit a flow
All ears on me when it's my time to unload
I spit fire as ashes come out of my dome
Lyrical ingenuity leaks out of my bones
Passaic is my thrown
Up from the minors I'm straight up home grown
Jersey be the mind state
This world like "fuck it" so I screw it then ejaculate
Charge the rapid gates
Of hell taken charge knocking over the walls of fait
I'm secular so I rely on my own faith
Skinny
Never really pumped the weights
I carry mine
Proceed to sign on the dotted line
Every time I speak I try to diversify
Through my rhymes
I speak softly as I'm killing a line
With small words can destroy a simple vibe
In every group there has to be a mastermind
So I drop a bomb like saddam that was triggered by time

9-7-07

-ELITE-

34

PRODIGY

THERE IS NO INTERMISSION, WHEN I SPEAK
WITH INTUITION.
THERE IS NO RETRIEVING, WHEN MY
CHARACTERS ACHIEVING. THERE IS NO
DECIEVING BECAUSE MY EXISTENCE IS
LEGITIMATE.
NOTHING ARTIFICIAL IN THE WAY I CARRY
MYSELF, THATS LITERAL WHICH INCLUDES
EVERYTHING FROM MY STYLE TO MY
LITERATURE
I KEEP IT ME, MENTALLY AND PHYSICAL, TRUE I
KEEP IT G. FOR ME THAT'S CRITICAL
WHEN YOU CAN REVERSE A THOUGHT BY DOING
NUTTIN BUT HEARING THE VOICE IN YA HEART
REBIRTH LIVE THIS CURSE
WIT'A SPARK TRY TO SEE LIGHT EVEN THOUGH
MOST OF THE WORLDS IN THE DARK. THESE
WATERS HAVE SHARKS. MANY ARE MAKING
IMPACTS, MOST ARE LEAVING A MARK. IM NOT
SAYING IM SMART
JUST AWARE OF MY SURROUNDINGS
ASTOUNDING ACCOMPLISHMENTS ARE
OVERSHADOWED BY TRAJEDIES. My FLIGHT
REDUCES CALORIES. EVERY FIGHT PRODUCES
CASUALTIES IM WRITING NOVELTIES THAT
WILL ONE DAY BE PUBLISHED SO YOU CAN ALL
READ MY HISTORY.
TREASUROUS SCRIPTURES INSCRIPTED IN MY
CONCEPTION. INTELLECTUAL STRUCTURE
THAT IS THE BRAIN NO MISCONCEPTIONS. EL
PRODIGIO DE LA ESCRITURA INDIFFERENTE
CUANDO SE TOCA EL TEMA DE RELIGION. CREO
EN DIOS, BUT IM AGNOSTIC CUZ THERE IS NO
WAY OF KNOWING EVERYTHING THERE IS TO
KNOW
I MAKE MY OWN JUDGEMENTS CUZ THAT DAY IS
COMING. WE MUST BE PREPARED FOR IT, WHEN
IT DOES WHO WILL START RUNNIN.
-ELITE-

9/11

I stared out the third floor window
2001 junior year
I stood in the hallway late to class
Shocked
All I saw was smoke
I felt the panic and worry of a nation under attack
The impact was felt
The heartbeats were pounding
It was felt loudly like the planes crashing
Every monitor spoke the tale of the events of that day
An unprecedented attack on the free world
Fighter jets flew over our school
Terrified
The eyes showed fear
The perpetrators were never revealed
But how can the free world allow such an invasion I thought
Was it another case of "waking up a sleeping giant"?
Was history repeating itself?
After the ambush at Pearl Harbor
School was not the same again that year
As the phones were flooded with bomb threats
Why was somebody wasting so much energy trying to bring us down?
Was it years of bullying that finally got to someone's heart?
I guess when you believe in something so strongly
You're willing to fight for it
And when you're willing to fight for something, you're willing to die for it
Therefore, we are willingly and unwillingly fighting for a cause
The scars will remain engraved in my mind
Of a day when we were compromised
Weather you blame our own leader or believe in the terrorist scheme
You deserve what you receive
I rather live for freedom and stay alive to be free

-ELITE-
2/10

"9"

Atomic number of fluorine
The number nine
As in the right fielder
Signs couldn't be any clearer
It generally takes nine months to create a life
I'm on cloud nine when I write
Birth
Nine lives describes a cats worth
Nine wives
I describe my life in nine rhymes
Word to the wise
On the streets at the blink of an eye
A nine can take your life
Ghetto slang symbolizing homicide
Pistol victims
Nine original planets in our solar system
Nine
Like Roger Maris' retired jersey
Leading the yanks to victory
Fame
Like the nine players on the field
Ready for a nine inning game
Engine engine number nine is the train
On that New York, transit line
When I'm really dressed up
I'm just assumed "dressed to the nines"
Punishment
Like a cat-o-nine tails suggest
The ninth book of the bible
Kings
Demands power and respect
Ninth commandment teaches about bearing false witness
against your neighbor
Correct
My daggers and swords write sharp
Nine chapters on the mathematical art

Smart
An ancient sacred symbol like the nine-pointed star
Ghetto fabulous a part of the slang
Nine original members of the *Wu-Tang Clan*
Shaolin
Lyrical morphine
Catastrophies
The ninth month brought the biggest attack I'd ever seen
Or witnessed
2001
Nine is the symbol of immutable truth
This is no gimmick
I'm writing history in lyric
I'm often a cynic
But I know nine is the highest single digit
Therefore, I become a critic
Any number multiplied by nine results in digits adding to nine
Unraveling your mind
Simply put, its one of a kind
It is defined
In everything from technology to astronomy
Nine major openings to the body
The number of harmony
Virgo comprising of three trinities
Jesus appears nine times to his disciples
Resurrection
Expired after the ninth hour
Perfection
Face your fears
The Trojan War lasted nine years
Let's be quite clear
Anything of nine components is called an ennead
I have your mind glowing
Nine-west clothing
I'm casting out nines
Giving sight to the blind
I weighed nearly nine pounds
As I patiently waited in moms wound
For nine months
Important Buddhist rituals involve nine monks
Nine

Associated with the Chinese dragon
Nine
Forms of the dragon
Symbolizing magic and power
Nine
One less then a dime
To remind you that you don't have to be a ten to be fine
Nine ball like the standard pro billiards variant
Passionate evening
Ninth Avenue in Manhattan
Nine Gods and Goddesses
In the Egyptian, Celtic, Greek, and Christian myths
Important
Like the nine worthies
9 jerseys
Of Parker Tony
Knicks fan but I don't hold grudges
U.S Supreme Court sits nine judges
Carson Palmer, Tony Romo, Mcnair or Drew Breeze
All QBs
9
The "nine days"
Nine is unlucky or lucky
Significant in Norse mythology
Hot like the rays of the sun
My minds on nine
Even though my favorite number is one

-ELITE-

Revised from 9/07

3/10

AUTOBIOGRAPHY

AN A TO Z ABOUT ME

Agnostic American
Analytical ambassador
Ambitiously anger's an afterthought
Alphabetical animal
Answers are automatically and anxiously amplified after all
Acknowledge aftermaths alphabetically
Atrocities
Blasphemy
Better brother
Become better
Baneful
Brave
Bravado becomes benign
Best belligerent brain
Brutally bright
Clever concise
Casually cocky
Cautious caring compassionately
Charitable
Cherishes company
Courageously captivating character
Causing comradery
Charismatic
Cool calm collective
Cynical
Completely clean collaboratively contemplative
Carelessly competitive
Circumstances create casualties
Contemporary
Cold calculative
Curiously corrupt
Courteous
Conservative controversial carnivore
Delusional
Diligent
Direct descendant
Disciplined Dominican
Determined

Deceptive
Dangerously dope
Diverse
Dominoes destroyer
Doomsday Dillinger
Dark De La Rosa
Day light damager
Deliciously done
Dictionary dissector
Durable dancer
Dynamic dangerous death defying
Eccentric
Energetic example electrifying
Elusive equality
Elegant enigma
Extraordinary excellence
Extremely enticing entertaining
Fiend for food
Favorable Flavorable
Forever flavorful
Focused
Fearless feline
Ferocious
Fearsome
Forgiving
Fearing failure
Ghetto genius
Generous giving gentleman
Genuine genes
Guillotine glowing green
Grown guaranteed
Girth growing greatly
Genetically geared
Gentle giant
Gangster guru
Grammars geniously great
Guerrilla going ghost
Gentle groomed
Host
Heroically humble
Hilarious humanitarian

Handsome
Hairiness' hereditary
Humility hits home heavily
Hispanic heritage
Heavenly handwriter
His handwritten histories have hieroglyphics
Intellectual individual
Instinctive
Intuitions intense
Insanely innovative
Impactful insights inspire incredibility
Jealous
Jerk jokingly
Jumpy
Jeffrey jayces just Jeff
Joyous just jest
Justifying justice
Jagged jersey journalist
Jock jeans
Keen
Knowingly knowledgeable
Kindhearted
KKK killer
Knickerbocker
Kissing king
Lean
Legit low-key Latin lover
Lyrical lyricist
Loving life's levels
Learning life's lessons
Literatures lava
Lectures leaving legacies
Liberal
Lady liberty
Lonely
Local literary legion
Legitimate listener
Literally
Major mind-state majestically
My mayhem mystifies
My madness makes my mind meditate

Mysterious
My message motivates movement
My messages movement makes maximum mental melodies
Masterfully
Mental marathon man
Misunderstood menace
Metropolitan
Minor meltdowns
Metaphorical maniac
Mediator
Mature memorable motor mouth
Managerial maneuvers must maintain
Mainly motivate
Merengue
My music
Machismo
Navigates
Never negative
Not
"Niggas" nothing new
Nigger's naïve
Nostalgic
Necessary
No nun
Natural nympho
Nocturnal
Nice New Jersey native
Noticeable
Nobody's nightmare
Newcomer
Neglects nicotine
Often overwhelmed
Own opinions on omnipresent omnipotence
On point ordinarily
Optimistic occasionally
Outspoken
Observant
Out of options
Onsite open ordinary
Official
Psychological

Piffed prophet
Potentially philosophical
Papers profit
Poverty's property
Punctual precise polite pretty professional
Poet
Poems precious
Permanent phenom
Presentably poetic
Postures problematic
Poetry's perfections paint pictures
Powerful presence presents poison
Planets problems persist per person
Perplex
Procrastinator
Playfully proud
Profound
Partner protector
Plead prayers
Prioritize painfully
Quick quiet quasar
Quality qualifies quest-fully
Real reserved
Respectful
Rugged rare raw
Relentless
Relatively raunchy
Ruthless renegade
Rational Reader
Rhythmic rhymer
Slick
Silent striker
So stubborn
Sick speech
Slick speaker
Street swagger
Somewhat spiritual
Seldom scared
Straight savage
Samaritan
Silky smooth

So sick style
So serious
Sarcastic sabbatical
Simple serene
Smart sometimes syndical
Tactical
Tall thoughtful truly talented
Tools thicker than thick
Thoughtful
Timely traditional
Taking thoughts traveling through time
Theoretically
To the thinking tomb
Terrestrial
Tough tamed tiger
Uncool
Uncut underrated uncle
Understandably unique
Underground
Underbelly's underappreciated
Ultimately untouchable
Unities utterly urgent
Unpredictable unprecedented
Understood
Uncontrollable
Very versatile
Vulnerable
Vamos vanish vanity

Viciously venomous
Verbal vigilante
Wild wrestling watcher
Warrior
Warm wicked word wizard
Writer who's wondrous
With wit
Willingly wants winning wickedly
Writing weaponry
Xenon
X-man
X-rated
Young Yankee
Yes yesterdays youth
Yup yearning yucky
Zap zilch zero
Zoned zealous zombie
Zigzag zig

-ELITE-

VENTING OUT

I take pride in being well kept
Most deft
I use to judge women strictly on the size of the chest
But a man realizes there is more to the mind then just breast
Nothing but truth inside the jests
Like a guillotine severing heads
Like a super morphine
Bringing you back from the dead
I am taking the liberty of speaking for all men
Blocking the actions of histamine, I am anti
Although I am forever against you, I'm an ally
Coming from the blindside
The wrong side of the trackside
I see fear I see death
Yet everything in between
At the end of the tunnel, I see me
In the flesh
Yes
I'm talking to you
That's anyone not understanding my point of views
I can be spiritual in my own way
I just don't need you telling me what I can or what I can't say
I speak Spanish, English, and truth all fluent
My flags Dominican American are almost congruent
Both with the red, white, and blue in it
I systematically influence
Freedom of speech cannot be deprived
I hate ignorant minds accepting the lies
Mystified
Following the blind with your eyes open wide
Instead of taking advice from the wise
Challenging your minds is why I write
Do or die
Never faking the style
To compromise is like telling a lie so never mind

-ELITE-
6/11

48

RICE AND BEANS

There is more to me then meets the eye
There is more to me than just rice and beans
A loud mouth Dominican with a soul quite serene
Btw, I also eat pasta, Chinese and such
It just so happens that most of the time,
I'm gonna' have rice and beans
For dinner, I'm probably having rice and beans
Don't judge me by my good hair, my love for hot sauce, my tolerance for spice but,
Rather for my creativity, my ingenuity, my insight, my style
Swagger
Always on point and precise
Both my flags are red blue and white
Always for equal rights
Soul food and pizza slice
At the end of the day, I'm still eating beans and rice
Strength is my inner light
My Latin pride is a part of my life
We are the only type
That can go in your fridge, grab anything, and mix it with rice
Then blow the toilet up in the middle of the night
I'm more then just a cute Spanish guy
Latino
Full of myself
Who can merengue and bachata too
But I also have rhythm and blues
Rich in traditional views
Give me some fried foods
Mysterious eyes
I'm eating spice
But you look past and see the rice
Give me the chili

The bean sauce
The toilets being bombarded
I'm discretely soft
With a hardcore
Nice and mean
Precise and clean
Never what you might think you have seen
But forever ever always eating that rice and beans

-ELITE-

10-7-09

FRAGILE LION

He use to think that his shit didn't stink
In reality, he knew his spit wouldn't stick
He often figured he was "all that"
When in reality he wasn't jack
He played this tough character on the outside
But on the real, he was fragile and weak on the inside
He was insecure
To him very obscure
No nonsense
But 100 pounds soaking wet so he was self conscious
Hard to read he was everything but
Scared of commitment he would often fall victim to lust
He once had a goal of sleeping with 30 women by the age of 30
In which time he would decide to settle down "early"
Girls would come around, play around
He was well ahead of schedule
But he had standards don't get it twisted
His moral fiber would play out in most predicaments
He didn't trust too many people his loneliness would show
But when he gave his friendship it was 100% blow for blow
His previous experiences with women had him cold hearted
But his desire to procreate had him jump started
Wanting a family was a scarce reality
But he didn't want to be the man his dad was so he rejected
love
Knowing that whenever he chose to commit it would be
enough
Enough pussy hopping it was time to grow up
The fear of failure all of a sudden had struck
For he'd known at this stage of his life it could only make him
humble
All he ever wanted to do was be himself and never stumble
Never selfish but no one could ever tell
His good deeds were never publicized
He preferred to maintain his business discrete and wouldn't
accept otherwise
He would never compromise his attitude nor swagger

Being unique is something he took pride in as wise
Authentic, open minded and very competitive
One of his flaws was that of thoughts that were negative
Hated to lose never took it lightly
Sports minded, character polished always spoke politely
But when it mattered the most he always kept it real
He would drown his loneliness and sorrows in his rhymes
He listened to conscious rap analyzing the poetry line for line
Digesting each one at a time
His street slang and verb usage would sometimes stir
controversy or raise flags
But "that's how I am" would be the final verdict
Ghetto poet
Never took nothing for granted
He was family oriented
His Yankee fitted permanently slanted
Low-key but always about action
Always romancing but was never one to chase
Kept to himself so writing was his escape
Homebody couch potato innocent minded
Not an ounce of evil in his body watching pro-wrestling was
his hobby
Didn't accomplish much but through his poems he was
successful
A quiet genius amongst stars he was special
But lazy
At least some thought he was, but he would put himself down
Even a smile to him would be an upside down frown
He had a difficult time even showing his pearly whites
For being reserved, was just a way of life
Military style
His dad would whoop his behind
So as a grown man he's learned to live through the pain and
struggle with a serious face
Hoping that one day people will know'em and not judge'em
Growing up with 5 relatives in a small apartment
Killing roaches and rats routinely at least they had a carpet
Nothing luxurious but they always had a hot plate
He would look at his gay cousin and hope to one day never be
that way
Homophobia sank in but he doesn't discriminate today

Only one friend most of his life Jose
He was never good enough to partake in activities so he chose
To sit back and watch the rotation of the globe
Breath in and out using his big nose
Staying alone with no where to go
He wrote this self-criticism in hopes to be embraced
Knowing some poor decisions in the past caused him a lot of disgrace
His mind never accepted the ideas of others
He could not conform
He made his own conclusions because he believed himself the most
Never a follower
Never a criminal
But he once stole a bag of chips from the bodega
He was creative
Of the world a native
Violence and drama was just something he hated
His main weakness was vagina
But it would leave him sedated
This is an autobiographical of actual factual
So as you go into "his" mind in this self-eulogy
Be advised with no lies that the "he" was me

-ELITE-
9-14-10

HOME SWEET GHETTO

Socio ecological issues thrive in the ghetto
Our social economies added by our poverty multiplied by
casualties subtract the street pharmaceutical industry, neglect,
and negativity plus our endangered mentality and equal our
population
In the ghetto
The jungle is the streets
The struggle is the concrete
Poverty is all the teary eyes see
Strength from within to one day set you free
They tell you the glass ceiling is unreachable
They're liars
It's just difficult to climb over it when it's covered in barb wire
Only the strong survive
Our social, legal, and economic pressures
Make us a "minority" in the slums on the other side of the
tracks
Records indicate that those who escape the wrath are prone to
surviving and striving as warriors
My writing's the tool in which I'll fly to the sky
The onlookers from outside give us a stereotypical stare
We glance back not giving a damn of a care
Biased treatment
Relentless
Never say die but ruggedly raw attitudes the norm
Firm and steady footsteps as crushed roach eggs get stuck in
your shoes
The comforting sounds of the sirens set the mood
The sweet cries of the neighboring reflect the truth
Real life is outside your window
The TV set displays a mere fantasy
An illusion
You can taste the hardships and restrictions like the spice and
seasonings in your Goya taste buds
The urban hoods populated by the intellectual thugs
Whose goals involve monopolizing the block by all means
using their conglomerates
Impoverished disadvantaged criminal minds with the belt

buckle below the waist proud
Counting every last dollar like bodies but our souls are rich
The industry cats are super stars in their eyes but the reality's thick
The dark knights come out once the dark lights run out
But when the sun rises and the blood, sweat, and tears dry up
The smoke dust clears and you awaken
Alive
A stronger being
Its home sweet ghetto
-ELITE-
2-10

MY ESCAPE

Notorious for my lines
But deep down inside my life's notoriously in decline
I escape the world with rhymes
A paragraph at a time
In my mind, the world is mine
So I sit back recline
As the dark night shines
Feel the bright light from the moon sending chills down my
spine
Five letters that I choose to define when I write
E.L.I.T.E
In my mind is the place to be
Every time when I lace a sheet
On my grind when the pencil leaks
Come inside and face the heat
As I express my thoughts onto precious sheets

-ELITE-

I'M THE TYPE

I'm the type to take allergy medicine with beer
Then drive home drowsy unable to steer
Often times I can't hear
Cuz I'm the type to zone out
Let my mind wonder thru time, space, and fear
I'm the type that's instrumental with my mentals
I'm the type to get jealous bug out and wild out
When I see you with a dude and you *aint* even my girl or my
spouse
I'm the type that loves to eat white rice
Throw some beans and a meat and it hits the spot every night
I rock silver not gold
I'm just that type
I like big booties, sports, food,
I'm the type that loves to write
I'm often moody
Type nice
I read, drink, but I'm type light
I'm the type to analyze
Open mind, not circumcised
Not religious no ones opinions but mine
I'm just that type
My business exposed I don't like
Real reserved I'm that type with the mystery eyes
Straightforward down to earth dude
Many flaws but forever I stay true
Trend setter no Mohawk
No ass showing my own style
Polo with matching fitted my profile
Humble quiet at times so loud

Basically
I don't care bout hype
Don't care what your like
Just keep it real at all cost at all times at all price
That's my type
I can go from *"WU-TANG"* to Jordan Sparks
From merengue to "LINKIN PARK"
My diversity is as scary as Jason or Freddy
I'm the ghetto type that holds his heart on his sleeve
Gets heart broken then takes out his frustrations on a sheet
I'm warm and cold
Grumpy and happy
Nevertheless, to myself I'm just *that type*

-ELITE-

10/08

WHEN IM GONE

When I'm gone, I'll still be alive
But will anybody take the time to find me or bother to say hi?
Will anybody cry?
Will anybody cherish the good or bad times?
Will anybody continue to believe the blind lies?
Nobodies going to die
But will anybody sit back and stop to think why?
There were things I never thought twice to try
Gave second chances cause the heart deserves to survive
Made wrong things right
Pride myself on being someone in which you can rely
Maybe the choices I made were not always so bright
And my mood could change from the morning to night
But when I'm gone is anybody going to dare to blink twice?
Is anybody going to care to think nice?
Is anybody going to be fair or polite?
Will anybody care to think twice?
Or is my reputation going to fail and be trife?
When I'm gone, will I even get a hug?
Will anyone be mine?
Will I get a smile, a pound, or will they give me the eye?
Will I get a positive or negative vibe?
If I declare "peace"! Will I receive a reply?
When I leave I won't be looking or coming back
When I am gone
No lie we will find out who is on whose side
Plus I won't have anything to say but just a simple goodbye

9-9-2009
Elite

MY PHILOSOPHY

Biochemistry
Thinking philosophically and physiologically
Trying to uncover my anatomy
My mind state's capacity
Goes beyond the galaxies universities
The soul's infrastructure
Prettier then any cosmetic surgery
Fuck superficiality
Your insides are greater then any form of authority
Higher seniority
Realer then mythology
Deeper then monogamy
Harder then geometry
Ever long lasting forever like geology
All over the earth's surface like geography
No casualties
Check your glossary
My vocabulary's itinerary's more valuable then commodities
My moral properties
Infiltrate your spiritual qualities
I neglect, reject, and go against
Every single one of your prophecies
With integrity no lack of variety
Monotony
Worship yourself because your church is in your psychology
The future is now is my prophecy
Conspiracies only exist in your mind
Like Socrates, make your own theories
Hell fire and brimstone
That's a thinking mans philosophy

-ELITE-

LEARNING TO ADAPT

I use to have a very hard time trying to adapt
To the chit chattering ways of all the gossiping rats
Conniving
To the point that my spirit would collapse
My demeanor would snap
My shell would crack
I was already forewarned but I just couldn't react
I wasn't used to it
It's nobody's business who I did or didn't hit
But shit
I had to cope with it in a serious way
How you know we hooked up when it just happened yesterday?
The rumor mille had me fucking a different chick everyday
I was a pimp
So I just sat back and ate it away
The stories and lies had opened everyone's eyes
All I wanted to do was be employed in my mind
But shit
I sucked it up and came to work right on time
Nobody to trust, so on myself I relied
Mental strength at the end of the day was the prize
Not knowing how to brush shit off could've been my demise
So I cried
But my tears were invisible
Because my interior wouldn't show
My pride is impenetrable
My exterior hides what I'm feeling inside
The sound of the keyboard was what I used to distract
So while you're staring at stone frozen in time
Like when Lot's wife looked back
I'm realizing that the strength of my heart will never seize to
adapt

-ELITE-

9-23-10

61

<u>NEVER COMPROMISED</u>

I can't compromise myself anymore then Mario can stop
rescuing
The princess
Like an eagle can stop spreading
Its wings
Like the sun can avoid setting
I sing
This song of self righteousness
Money, power, respect can't buy my soul
Nor my empowerment
My character cannot be purchased nor compromised
It's measured and acknowledged through my knowledge's
knowledges
Positive
That's what my knowledge is
The concept of being you is underrated
Underappreciated
Overlooked and never promoted
When it comes to being like the rest of the following lambs
My style gets demoted
Demoted by self
Cause I choose to refuse to include to induce
Anything other then originality in my person
Creativity lurking

My person is all I have at the end of the day
So I stay true to it
Rich or broke like MC Hammer
I'll be too legit to quit
And so I
Walk with my swagger
Dress with my style
Speak with my unique tongue
Display my Dominican pride
Express myself with my blessed, original, gift
Art
Love
Poetry
I'm me
That's all that I can be
And I won't be compromised no matter what you people think

-ELITE-

10/10

MISUNDERSTOOD

My hearts so cold, I feel so old
I let go of the single thing I had
Now I have no soul
Before I used to glow
Now I feel as dark as a shadow
All alone
In a universe full of ghouls and ghosts
Sometimes the world just doesn't feel like home
Therefore, I quarantine myself in my dome
Only to open up to the page
Because I don't trust a soul
My sole purpose is to remain enclosed
I periodically go insane
And start to think with a killer's code
I'll pump your brain out
Pop your veins out
Snap off your umbilical cord before you're even born
Drain out your blood vessels
Insane route
Mind thoughts are maniacal at times
But they never play out
I shout and my sanity wins out
Cynical
I just write and escape out
Erase out
The sinister and suicidal mind state out
My consciousness
The worlds got me this way

-ELITE-

10/08

I'M

I'm hesitant
I'm cautious
I'm relevant
I'm nauseous
Irrelevant
I'm everything
I'm just me
I'll make you laugh
I'll make you cry
I'll make you smile
I'll make you die inside
I'll let you fly
I'll bring you alive
I'll take away your pride
I'm the one that won't let you sleep at night
I'm just that type
To make your eyes shine
To fill your guts with butterflies
To uncover the blinds on your feelings when they hide
I'm never shy
I never lie
I cause pain
I cause joy
I cause fear
I exploit
I can annoy
I'm good
I'm evil
I'm what the world needs
I'm bad
I make you happy and sad
I make you lose your mind
I'm one of a kind
I'm what people seek
I'm what people fear
I make you heart leak
I make you hear and see
Things that normally wouldn't appear

I'm what's involved hen marriage is near
I influence cupid's wrath
I'll make you give the last bit
Of food no matter how hungry you are
I conquer all
I'm eternal
I'm like the flight of a dove
I'm from above
I'm just me
I'm love

-ELITE-

1-7-09

THE UNKNOWN

My shaft of sunlight
Like a golf club or hammer
Hole in one bright
Injecting pleasurable pain
Like a locomotive train
Super sonic but
Not electronic
Blood flow makes it stiff
Defying science
Thick
Big head and the women love it
Dollar dollar bills
You need plenty of it
Feeding utensil
Food for your mental
Essential
Good nourishment
Credentials
Hard to ignore
Explore smooth silk
Make your bones strong
Got milk
Sticks out with excitement
Strands of hair do not exist
Preciseness
It'll put you to sleep like a sedative
Induced hormone like estrogen
Volcanic eruption
Lava burning thru your skin
Melting your person
Leaving you seduced is the purpose
No remorsing
Louisville slugger
Hitting homeruns out of the park
Like mating season after dark
Reaching home base with a slide
Cloud nine valentine
When the magic stick brings you to climax time
Forensic evidence left behind
-ELITE-

THE MESSAGE

Your infrastructure is a liability
Degrading
My inability to move on is mentally depraving
Headaches
The homeless on the corner consumed by his mistakes
The vain and shallow concerned with jewels seen
The pain on the streets eyes is what fuels me
When I write I catch frostbite
I catch a cold while you're catching feelings
Chilling
But my written is hot
Feelings sentimental
They're instrumental when I write on the spot
Lyrical nine
Ink cartridges from my pen have been shot
I'm everywhere
Been wrongfully accused but my name will always clear
Slice of orange in my blue moon glass
Unlocking the past
The last will come first and the first will come last
I've done plenty of wrong
Dark memories tainting my soul
But another man's wife I will never unrobe
I have never been that cold
Therefore, I'm kept alone with nobody to hold
So I shrug off my shoulder and move forward as my story is
told
The truth will always unfold
As it sets me free
Truth that only my eyes can see
Secluded from the world
I have my own ways of expressing myself
My feelings are kept hidden oftentimes until they melt
No hitters when I'm on the mound
On solid ground
I show my love with a simple fist pound
I'm humble now
So don't judge me

Until the message sinks in
Disguised as a blessing
What I received the night the car flipped
My mind tripped
I met death and gave her a kiss
But I was free
Crawled out white fitted was clean
Glass cut on my leg
Alive
But the experience was scary
Surreal
Speeding on a highway with a drunk driver was crazy
But it saved me
That is why I don't let females drive its paranoia
Never take for granted the air you breathe
Please
Realize your only praying in times of need
Best believe it just wasn't my time to leave
Everything changes with time but until then I'll just breathe
Pay attention to the life you lead
Exceed succeed but never let your mind freeze
To my cousin
Even if you're gay, I still love ya
Now I'm relieved
Message across
Mind is at ease

-ELITE-

4-14-10

Super lirica

Super lirica
La calidad y cualidad de mi material es imperial
Super lirica
No digo nada que no sea la verdad
Super lirica
Es veridico mi mentalidad es extensiva hasta lo ultimo
Soy super lirico
Muchas mentiras he visto
Sentido
Muchos corazones partidos
Heridos
Muchas personas perdidas
Solo sin amigos
Mi hermana me apoya
En el fondo es mi abrigo
Sencillo
No soy tiguere Ni ando con corillo
No soy perfecto pero tengo mi estilo
Individual
Original
Aunque no lo crean soy el mas perpetuar
El mas virtual
Dios patria libertad
Super lirico

-Elite-

9-14-10

DIVERSIFIED INK

I'm diverse when I write
I'm diverse when I write because I can take a black pen, put it
to a white paper and father different cultures of words.
Different colors are born different lectures are learned
Different trees are burned
Very few stones left unturned
I have a gift not a curse
To turn words into thoughts and those thoughts into verse
I'm diverse
Because when I write, I tell a story of a world that gets worse
I have yet to scratch the surfaces turf
But thru my scriptures I'm alive forever one with the universe
I try to keep it real, because I know bout the truth and it hurts
My heart pounds liquid pain
The rage burns with intensity
When I write that fire translates into diversity
Authentically never generically
Manifestation of lyrical war within me
Leaving pivotal scars internally
That reach out for centuries across seas and galaxies
Thoughts last and travel thru light years
I'm quite clear
When I say my writing diversity has integrated with the
hemispheres
It's simply just too much for me to bear

-ELITE-

1-29-10

FIRST IMPRESSION

You see a backwards cap and assume I'm a thug
You see long hair and goatee and call me a scrub
Meantime my insides are never shown
Never exposed
My soul wears a tuxedo and acts grown
It stands alone but sits on a thrown
You see the mysterious eyes and wonder what's inside
There's always more then meets the visuals
You won't know if I'm spiritual
I won't show if I'm liberal
I'm real to myself at all times and that's literal
I take fake cats weasel roaches rats
Snakes
Block them from my mental state
Firm handshake
The thought of snitches hotwires my brain cells
I ditch'em in my mind I throw'em in ditches
With stitches but I cool out
With no doubt I'm true to self
With total disregard for all other else
My presence is felt

-ELITE-

7/08

A DAY IN A LIFE

Corona bottle caps popping off
Reminiscing
Realizing life is harder then soft
Contradictions
Taking a bite of a burger
No time for weight loss
Writing rhymes to pass time
Can't escape being lost
It's all in a days work
Taking orders from a boss
No remorse
Trying to avoid charley horse
Main priorities to get by of course
Police sirens music to my eardrums
Memories come
History repeats itself when you think about one
This very date is rare
It won't again soon come
Looking forward to when car payments are done
So I sit back watch the tube as the poison injects
Reflect
Face booking Hanes showing thinking bout good sex
Select thoughts
That'll make the day a success
Divert
Avoiding sobriety analyzing tranquilizing
Being comfy comes first
My glance is covert
Styling profiling is routinely the look
Following suit
Yankee fitted matching the boots
In all colors
Going forward like rooks
A chariot to transport my words
Rice and beans on the plate
As the chicken marinates
Hot sauce
Living poor mind state

Rich be the thoughts
Rebelling
Pushing the envelope with force
There is always a cause
Serving justice to self
Give me a round of applause
On occasion sipping the brew
Telling the truth
Looking up at the sky every night with no clue
My words reflect views
Of a day in a life
Searching the mind of the acute
Eat it, swallow and digest it
Analyze
To understand you have to dissect it
Synchronize

-ELITE-

10-10-10

I WANNA WRITE

I wanna write until there's no more ink
I wanna make the pen bleed verse after verse
Without a single blink
I wanna write about art, love, philosophy,
Anything deep
I wanna make you think, learn, analyze
And keep reading
I wanna make you visualize my words
Spiritualize memorize my enterprise
Catch a breath then become breathless
As you, digest what I express
I just wanna write
It's a passion like fruit
It's a hobby, a life form, all the above
In my pjs, with a hoodie
At work, anywhere I keep it gully truthfully
If I can possibly change the world
With my words I'ma be heard
Change the globe send a message
Without weapons make ya' head spin
A writing veteran
This is fighting medicine
To boost your adrenaline
Afterwards you need Excedrin
I wanna write as Steinbrenner wants to win
I need to write as a fish needs a fin
I have to write, as a mermaid has to swim
Like a bum needs a home or aids needs a cure
Like I need a Shorty, I gotta write for sure
I need to write as if darkness needs light
Like a plane needs flight
Like a virgin is tight
Like the blind need, sight like left and wrong needs a right

Like Samsung needed hair for might
Like my stomach always in, need of a bite
Like a boxer needs a fight
It makes my day and sunlight shine bright
I compare it to life
I just wanna write

-ELITE-

10/08

VIDEO GAME MIND STATE

I use to dream of waking up to a room full of video games
Every game ever made
Every system known to man
Instead
I would wake up to my super Nintendo

All my friends had Play stations
Or something with 32 or 64 bits and higher
However, me? Nah
I had a super Nintendo
Mine had 16 bits of graphics
Nevertheless, it was super!

Yea saving the princess got tired and old after a while
As it went from taking an eternity
To saving her in 30 minutes
I mean, come on I knew all the shortcuts

Shit, all just for a kiss on the cheek and the chance to do it all
over again
At least I got to ride Yoshi but,
While my friends were busy stealing cars in Grant Theft
Or fighting wars and upgrading their Sony's and Nintendo 64s
I was eating mushrooms and getting big on my super Nintendo

Poverty's a bitch
But I will stick it to her raw
Who needs graphics and realism?
That is what real life is for
Therefore, I pause

Old school from the core
But Mario kept me humble
He kept me off the streets
I could not be by the corner store being "cool" or acting dumb
I was busy having to save princess Peach and the mushroom
kingdom
From Bowser

With my super powers and exceptional prowess

But there is always a moral to my madness
I don't follow the negative innuendos
Or the trendy trends
So go ahead with this mislead, misdirected society
I'll be instead playing my super Nintendo entertainment system

-ELITE-

6-29-10

SORE LOSER

Failing is not an option
But it's my biggest fear
Success keeps taunting me
It's ringing in my ear
Like an extreme phobia
Losing ignites a spark in my brain
That lights up and causes outrage
Flames and fights until I lose it
So I'm encaged
The thought of a loss no matter the consequence
Nor the size
The most minuscule of loses
Results in my demise
Total collapse enters my mind
It's serious
I need to win at all cost
Fee or free
It's just the competitor in me
It's almost a sin
Can never face defeat
So let the challenge begin

-ELITE-

4-27-10

SELF ASSURED

Do not confuse cockiness and confidence
In my mind, I'm the best poet alive and that's a positive
And through your eyes, I will stay relevant and prominent
And at the sky I'll grab a star and make it gas again
I keep my expressions trapped inside like the masked men
But that's irrelevant
Hidden
I'm often seen as a hooligan
But that's farthest from the truth
In reality, I'm known to cause a sweet tooth
I'm probably wrong
When I say I'm the greatest
Take it for what its worth
A lot of you are speaking knowledge
But it's mostly all dirt
Know I'm benevolent
Your minds for sale rite now I own it to rent
I have a great smile, but I keep it locked
Tucked away only for those who keep watch
Shocked
I'm like all styles combined
I'm like all minds in one
With every page I write
Another narrative is done
Another story is told
Another's interest is won

-ELITE-

4-28-10

WARRIOR

As the skies darken
And all hell materializes
I survive
Cause I'm a warrior

When emotions rampage
And my feelings are rushed
I live, learn, and strive
Cause I'm a warrior

I raise my hands to the sky
Pick my head up high
Even when I cry
I resemble a warrior

Mortals die
Immortals live forever
Warriors fight for eternity
Their spirits and legacies live on with no end
When all your energies spent
Blood, sweat, fear is indicative
Of a warrior

Victory lasts a lifetime
Excellence outlasts an eternity
A warrior symbolizes the ongoing struggle
For survival

Alarm clocks your wake up call
Laboring thru the day tripping but never fall
A lot of wasted fear
Many tasted tears

A renegade not giving a damn
Bout the morning
As long as his names held high
With no warning

As the skies open
The warriors bloom
The heavens capture the essence of
Ones true doom

-ELITE-
2/10

GUILLOTINE

UNOFFICIAL SYNOPSIS

I sever with blunt force
Handsome of course
I write with no remorse
I'm like a knight on a horse
When I write with no pause
Gunning straight for your thoughts
Cutting chase to the source
You find your minds often lost
When I describe what's on mind
It becomes a report
Distraught
My words intoxicate like Passaic's contaminated state
Pollution rate
Increases right from the gate
But still its home sweet home of the brave
I'm like a newborn
Pure
I'm like a man on his deathbed
With no cure
Often unsure
For the most part clear
That I will write until the ending is near

-ELITE-

VENOMOUS QUARREL

Metamorphosis through my rhymes they cause hypnosis
Honesty with just the right dosage
Of fibs
They travel through your mind and form explosives
No hoaxes
Humility is born with
I lead like Moses
Parting seas
Never follow the lead
Most people we look up to never display heroics
They are just shallow
Urban legends myths like sleepy hollow
I see beyond that
Go straight to the source like an arrow
Most mind states are narrow
Mine is open and it's lethal
No colors we all people
Regardless of see through
Christian, atheist, or clueless
We all equal
I emphasize this until it sinks in your cerebral
The cover of my book does not show a synopsis
You have to open it and uncover its purpose
Open closets and discover the corpses
Unlock the soul and determine the choices
That make who you are
For every cure, there's a poison

-ELITE-

9/08

FUTURISTIC QUATRAINS

Calamity falling from the sky
Famine and plague's destruction arrives
Microchips ruling the earth
Technology can't save what's been ruined at birth

Life drowning caused by water and wind
Luke 21 predicts the end of all things
Armageddon is near its clear thru whirlwind
Quakes shaking the world eternal resting

Immediate chaos overpowering fear and anxiety
Maximum carnage inevitable and irreversible catastrophe
Death and extinction created by man
Sickness no health while living in this land

One question remains
We look for answers in pain
Little time to rejoice
Did we ever have a choice?

Evil is to live as Devil is to have lived
The big dragon takes over
Incorporates his belief in one God
Currency marked by the symbol
Its purpose to breath fire as humanity sobs

It's beautifully horrible
21st century oracle
Speaking directly to God

Allow me to part seas
Like Moses did the red
But please don't erase my sins
Let me learn from them instead

-ELITE-

3-22-11

REINCARNATED SOULS

Staring into the skies
I see life
Reincarnated souls are the only things in sight
They roam
Even at night they see light
Darkness overpowers with the ability to shine bright
Precisely promising the weak with might
Negative forces are taking over this realm
Catastrophes unleashed while negativity overwhelms
Everything is left unanswered
Million questions through the mind get transferred
Seeing stars in the sky miles high wondering what holds them
up
If you can read this higher upper when will you enlighten us?
Trust the clues of your existence are not convincing me but
Every mystery needs to be solved
Every solution holds weight
Hate, love, memories, taste
Everything wastes
Everything that happens in this world is far beyond are control
Beings come and go
But only one thing remains
Were we poured into the earth like a cereal bowl?
While everything dies, the only things left behind forever are
reincarnated souls

-ELITE-

GRAMMATICAL EVOLUTION

This is for those who mistaken there's with theirs
Who except and don't accept
Who commonly put an I after an e
With that theory you won't achieve
Unless you're trying to perceive
Without the right spelling it's just a pet peeve
Quite endangering
Your youth is being influenced by text messaging
The emails and face booking is slowing our kids progression
Turning silent laughter into LOLs and "shock" into OMGs
The is now DA
And the unemployment goes up as our nations grades go down
Frown
Most importantly
I can't read or even see
A paragraph with fragments
Please seeds lets proceed to practice
In your head play it back
Lack of syntax
Go back and reread it
Make sure it's to and not too if your going somewhere
Repeat it
We have to be mentally prepared and not scared
For the decrease in talent and awareness
Beware of this
So correct your grammar not your grammer
Mean what you say but don't be mean when you say it
Let's share the soil that allows the seeds to give birth
Into plants and trees that inhabit the earth
Mental growth spurt
Recite it till your jaw bone hurts
Provide nourishments, oxygen, and air to breath
Don't mistake the leaves with leave
We need to live
Lets allow them to blossom lets start by correcting our speech

-ELITE-
10/10

SNOW FLAKES

Snow flakes
Landing on the pavement
Lyrical winter wonderland
An escape is my payment
The spirit of giving
Overwhelms my mind state
Despite the circumstance
The tree lights are bright
Street lights
Reflect the hustle and struggle
Of street life
Holidays, always on time and precise
Why do we need a "special" day to make our wrongs right
Or sing a song tonight
I think its mockery hypocrisy
This Santa clause never arrived for me
They lied to me
Society today accepts but also fights traditional qualities
And ideologies it's all conspiracies
Its all myths
But best believe my love will have me handing out gifts
Come the 25th
My wrath is like a hypocrites fit
I'm a misfit during holidays at times I feel like I just "miss
Christ"
I spit mist who the hell even invented Christmas
Snowmen are born
New friendships are formed
Hidden inside my hoodie the spirit keeps me warm
Shivering is only physical
The soul holds the typical
Norm of a cynical
Though my pockets are broke on the literal
To put a smile on a face is enough to keep the merry melodies
visible

12-09
-ELITE-

SOCIAL SECURITY

My social security administration
Preservation
Means not what you think
I'm thinking more like uplifting a nation
Egos second to none
Penultimate thoughts set up the last line beautifully
Splash ink furiously
We can't secure ourselves let alone our society
Government funding never reached me
Social security left my checks empty
Economic security has no relevancy
My income tax comes in the form of a dictionary
Because my words are worth more than anything monetary
The growling stomach of the cocky but humble
I write from hunger
I'm sure you would concur
Gas rises to $4 but I'm just a 9 digit number

-ELITE-

4/11

KNOWLEDGE

Knowledge is one
Born from the sun
Destructive like the shootings in Tucson
Gruesome
Poetic knowledge is explosive like the anatomy of a time or
atomic bomb
Infinite calm
To deal with all the miscellaneous harm
The worldwide inequality that we call home
Is crucial
Insecurity
In reality, it's just a small pond
The social disintegration is depriving our mentalities
Mediocrity is accepted as positivity
Total decadence its insanity
Knowledge is commercialized as inhumanity
While the poison is fed thru the Medias fatality
This is discrete profanity to the faint heart
In order to never allow our minds to grow
They exploit the flow
Propaganda
Being naïve and dumb seems to be the new way to go
Constructive criticism is allowed when I write
This is wisdom-bled ink thru my veins when I write
Materialistic instincts teach in vague
Thru lights of insight
Poetical ninja as I throw darts as your third eye
Like priests or pastors reading scriptures to the mentally blind
Manipulating your existence
And subliminally controlling your minds
There isn't a worse crime as they take your every dime
While the knowledge seekers get life for petty crimes
I write to free minds
From the lives of forgotten cities, I breathe shine
This is spasm
Mental orgasm
I write to beat and defeat time
My lies are truth even when they deny all proof

Encyclopedic views are inclined to dispute
Flourishing the Grandview of a shapeshifting orchid
Beautiful like Mona Lisa's self-portrait
Ignorance leads to self-hatred
Not knowing what is fact and fiction
Like Noah transporting every living organism preventing
extinction
An ark full of worldly and deadly contaminants forming
intuition
Released within a new system like biochemistry
Wisdom
However, what you read is not always the right depiction
Strategy
Brainwashing is the real infliction
That's why I spit six syllables of sick shit
Until it sinks in
In sync
Multidimensional metronome
Multitalented calligraphy
Collaterally thrown in as security
My mind is a depository
For mystery and history
Like banks holding your money
But collecting your interest
Running the world in secrecy
In the face of adversary
We now believe in polygamy
Diversified Christianity
Nothing like what was taught by our ancestry
Law 2 of the 48 laws of power
Make use of your enemies
Always think strategically
Is a tactical form of flattery
Silence is the best form of agony
It roars loudly
Bible paper is now used to role blunts
Now holy scriptures are written in the streets
Based on the struggle that is seen
Be careful what you read
Everyone is born but not everybody breaths
Everybody sleeps but not everybody dreams

You can count Zs or you're free to count sheep
Those are your choices when you're taught to be free
Thus, I'm looked at differently
For thinking independently
I'm distinct like the masons of the 15th century
My words are endless like an English dictionary
Knowledge is learned
Wisdom is knowledge manifested
Thru a wise dome
Words are chromium plated metal
Steel chromosomes
Melt them and they evaporate into thoughts
When you put'em to use they evolve into gold to elevate and
evaluate your soul
Search within for your throne
Perceptive mentality is precise
Wisdom is second to knowledge
But it takes all your knowledge to call yourself wise
It's never compromised
Together they form to comprise understanding
It is clear mental comprehension
You don't necessarily have to agree with my speech
But surely, you'll gain knowledge when you read what I speak
To the minds less developed
Like a 3rd world country's downfall economically
Generally speaking, industrialized nations vary socially
Social equity only exists with the existence of poverty
Mental properties collapse
Surpass those simple mindedly
I am an entity of light
Wisdoms passed on giving all of you sight
I am a quiet genius and it means quite a lot
Although I cant prove I am
You can't prove I'm not

-ELITE-

3/11

94

NAMELESS WILD CREATURES

Nameless wild creatures-interpret symbols
From their subconscious into symbols
Of the conscious –
Morphing into abstractions in each other~
Fracturing splintering and bleeding out
Into new strands for consideration~
Multiplying like bacteria
Infecting like viruses

Wild and nameless creatures
Shameless
Crossing a sea of deception
A seed of perfection planted
Instilled upon mere mortals
We form like a chimeran plague
We belong on this stage
But we are creatures of the universe

Populus vult decipi ergo decipiatur~
And so they perceive what they want
And take what they want~
Consuming until their fragile reality
Deluged upon them~
Waking them to the dreaming

Awaken to the unseen
To what the untrained eye sees
The third eye maximizes society's prophecies
Nameless creatures of the night arrive at harsh and wild
realities by daylight

Mercurial irregular beats
Creating ripples in its wake
Waves that wash over and reach out
Curious creatures steal closer
Drifting thru the waves
They sink deeper
Like a fisherman of the stochastic
It waits

Invisible to the world
Creativity is their fortress
Solitude is their company
Secluded for being ones own subordinate
Radically distinctive like the characteristics of an only
specimen
It awakes

-ELITE & WILD-

4/10

#23

You killed us time and time again with your jays
Your flawless finesse
Smothering defense
And impeccable grace
You knew how to make the best men look like a disgrace
Even jamming in space
Every Knicks fans nightmare
Shit, we should've one at least one title in the 90s
It was never fair
You made your second home Madison Square
Breath taking icon nicknamed after air
More legendary then a Reggie Miller
Soaring through the sky was the silent killer
Defying gravity, hot streaks insanity, flue like symptoms
couldn't stop this calamity
Spike yelling profanities
You made the #23 impossible to live up to
For no man can equal the king of the dunk
Master of the buzzard beater
With a magical sneaker
There's no game that you couldn't win even when playing dead
Hated to lose, sweat trickling down the signature bald head
A New Yorker breaking New Yorkers hearts
Every single time so we hated your guts
Smart
Calm cool collected demeanor as you shrugged your shoulders
with a smile
Cocky, tongue out to the side
Uncanniness wild
As we looked on with tears in our eyes
Although we couldn't stand you
We would've loved you on our side

-ELITE-
3/10

I TOO, RISE: ODE TO MAYA

I rise
The way you inspired those who heard your lullaby
I rise like the words from the page
In praise
To the girl with the diamond thighs
Ms. Angelou
I rise as if I will uplift my mind
The way you uplifted a culture
With a smooth descriptive array of rhymes
I rise like every soul who came up from the bottom
Who thru your eyes flew
Till they saw nothing but sky
Like a hot air balloon
I rise
With total disregard to negative vibes
From streets where lives are lost and found
Overcoming adversity, odds, and never looking down
To the depths of the galaxies
Back in time again
To a place where freedom was only a dream
So I reflect upon a nightmare
And wake up more serene

You can bring me down
Still I'll rise from the shadows
Deceit and hate will be
Targeted by my bow and arrow
Are you amazed at how I use my resourcefulness?
My swagger
To induce positivity
I rise
Mentally and physically
I attract like moths to light
Like my Latin flavor make your taste buds unite
As they collide
I continue to rise
Like hot lava from a volcano
Like the flight of a space probe
Like those who fought thru oppression
Like surviving the struggle of a great depression
Like weathering the heaviest of storms
Day or night
Yes
I too rise!

-ELITE-

5-4-10

APRIL SKILLZ

Slow days equal slow pay
In a cubicle all day
To provide food on my plate
My mood is, never hate
Times precious
Never late
I put the pen to the paper and let it marinate
It carries weight
The entire load from my mind is spilled when I concentrate
Allow me to reiterate
I never hate on the next
Hustle your best to get that Rolex
None materialistic
Birds eye view from the sky
Looking down on earth as it starts to dry
No more water we die
Nevertheless, I'm here to quench your thirst
Spoken word artist since birth
Every 24 hours pressure intensifies
Havoc and chaos begin to arise
Formations of hell on earth commence to materialize
Heaven must exist in our own minds
In order to survive
Lost souls travel thru endless time
This is poetry
Don't get it twisted with rhyme
The words just happen to coincide
It's an art form when I recite
Expressions when I write
Words that are tight
Flammable
They heat ice
Melt the ink
Then it dries up on the sheet
Hardcore thoughts originate from the streets
Actions reflect that which you have underneath
Your inner skin should be unique

I unleash dogs on copycats
Yankee fitted to the back
Tilted hat
Usually blue or black
Casual
No casualties
I'm true to that
Like the g-men pulling sacks
No cutting slack
Rearview mirror always looking back
Falling asleep can get your possessions jacked
Awareness must never be lacked
In this world full of rats
I write a bible of facts
Novel journals intact

-ELITE-

4-18-10

CEREBRAL WARFARE

My mind often travels thru time
Writing rhymes
Blowing up lyrical mines
Mental grind
Utilizing ingenious lines
Using a pen as a nine
Cerebral warfare becomes the crime
Speaking in metaphoric
Syllables catch your eye
All questions are rhetoric
Concentrated potency written in blind
Vitamins like the acid ascorbic
Ink and page side by side
Moving collaterally on a sheet parallel
To the finish line rapidly in sync
Vague thoughts are now extinct
Putting words together the perfect pictures complete
Mathematical scriptures
Adding up to intrigue
Painting portraits with mystique
Telling stories unique
Attractively sleek
Smooth criminal killing the mentally weak
Materializing the obsolete
As I'm speaking the street
Sneak the metaphors in while describing the sweet
Scent of the concrete
Makes you wonder to a place more serene
No vision to see
Thriving a word at a time
Mental collapse is all you can seek
As I travel thru minds

-ELITE-

4-27-10

102

WORDS FROZEN IN TIME

Hell will freeze over the day I stop writing my thoughts on a
sheet
That will be the day I fall asleep
And never wake up from a dream
That has never been seen
An autopsy on my mind only reveals what you read
My brain is the chamber that encloses the unseen
I arrive on scene with a scheme
My wordplay is the cause that leads you to believe
That you're smarter than you seem
I elevate your thought process to a higher level
Speech flow always sounds clever
Therefore, if I stop writing, your mind becomes severed
Never underestimate your self-esteem
Never
I express myself when I write the pen and paper's my team
Unique style with a twist comes from the genes
Poetic scheme
Instrumental
The castle gates open up I enter
The kingdom, kings and queens
Acknowledge the knighthood prestige
Quintessential
Ice cold words forever frozen in my mental

-ELITE-

10/08

EXPRESSION

Hypothetically speaking
I'm instrumentally reaching
Your ear drums
While you soul searching
As I'm teaching
Warrior stands alone with his sword
Excalibur's my pen
My words will inform
Attacks verbally tap a jaw leave you mentally scarred
Fighting thousand cold wars
Sky clears up a new sun is born
Thunder and lightning strike as I rise at dawn
While I raise my palms
Continue to weather the storm
In controlled but cataclysmic form
Brain cells dead by dawn
My molecules are far from norm
Wisdom is integrated in my vocabulary
Lyrical sanctuary
My escape is poetry
I awake my mind state relates the pain in me
Express sensitivity but hardcore explicitly
I abuse a dictionary splendidly
Every word flows accordingly like choreography
The syllables role off my tongue like musical symphonies
Sexual wizardry
Exposing the inner me
Poetical laboratory
Pre and post posthumous
Self anger management like alcoholics anonymous
My gentle soul can be hazardous
But always one hundred till infinity is reality
Those who are gelatinous parasitic tapeworms get defecated out
my anatomy
I force my own history of words like etymology

-ELITE-
10-09

INSECURITY

This fear kills me
Insecurities drill me
Preventing me from being,
Still me
Ironically the things that attract me
Usually scare me away
Therefore, I escape
To a place where I'm in solitude
Enclosure
Never one to follow or even look for exposure
A quiet soldier
A giant bolder disguised as a silent noble
Depression overtakes my anatomy
Not being able to control my anxieties,
My feelings or even my mentality
My frustrations often cause intoxication
Hallucinations of a world without misinterpretations
Not being able to feel what I want or even want what I feel
It is a rather irrational deal
Incomprehension at will
But still
I keep emotions bottled up inside
Isolated they hide
From the rest of society
Which in turn causes internal animosity
My yellow brick road
Leads to a wall
Too high for me to climb
Therefore, I get tired and fall
My eyes see but my minds blind
My hearts bias and my souls lost
In time
Meanwhile I am pushing everything away
That can potentially make me one day

-ELITE-

9/08

ACRONYM

MEANINGS:

Elegance
Live
Intelligence
Tremendous
Equality

ACTIONS:

Elevate
Learn
Inspire
Teach
Energize

AVOID:

Epidemics
Lust
Ignorance
Temptation
Extinction

-ELITE-

ALCHEMY

Turning metal to gold
Lyrical alchemist
Turning hot paper cold
Melting lava into coal
Reversing science
Time traveling
Writing skyscrapers in bold
Defining life stories told
Touching the sky with the one pen that I hold
Froze
Are your brain cells as they conjugate my verbs
Transitive while always in transition on the move
The words find the fountain of youth
Moving units exquisitely
Explicitly my lyrical content materializes instantly
Never out of place like historical context
Graphically telling stories prolifically
Evacuating the page realistically
With life like creativity
With consistency
With alchemistry
Everything else is irreversible irrelevant irrelevancy

-ELITE-

8-31-10

REGULATED FIENDS

Dirty urine
Intoxicated mind state
Failed the test of fait
The only things sober are these words
Lacing the page
Trapped
Incarcerated like an inmate
Correctional facility
Tryna conceal your escape
Insubordination
Existing by chance
Reckless intent
Endangerment of self, seams unavoidable
License and registrations a familiar phrase
Confusions inevitable
Your résumé shows no room for a raise
A fiend
Addicted to morphine
Stressed
Therefore, you become hooked on amphetamines
Even antihistamines
Preventing the sneeze
The television promotes every drug that you "need"
New ads show you what you must take to stay "clean"
But you only see filth
You keep tryna cure something
But you will always need help
Every symptom has a cure
But even the cures cause death
Never ending plagues
Surrounding the world of the unisex
Blood shot eyes
To relieve pain
Poverty
No resource for property
Over indulgence of narcotics
And they don't have to be illegal
Open up your medicine cabinet and find drugs that are legal

Cerebral
Brain washed by the system as they have a field day
The media feeds as the markets get paid
As we inherit the seed, even our eardrums bleed
Addicted to this noise and
As we consume their poison
That seed grows into death
Which we accept as inevitable
All the while, we are played as fools
For the fiends I refer to
Are all of me and you

-ELITE-

5-12-10

FIGHTING

Positive reinforcements
Empowerment is forcing
Society to fight for rights that exist no longer
Causing animosity, hazardous situations
The atmosphere is clear, but
This is only a mere
Dream
We must fight for
Be clean
Let us fight for a world more serene
Fight for a broader horizon
Expand your minds and views
Let's escalate our conscious
No nonsense
In this fight, let's bite like Tyson
Let's unify globally for a common democracy
Lets
Dig into our guts a little deeper
With might and fight
Let's start fighting for flight
Search within selves with razor sharp hindsight
Internal sunlight shines through our person
Blinds the opposing
Get a tight grip
Make a tight fist
Never quit
Show that fight from within
If you fall
GET UP!
Short, tall, or small
We fighting for a common cause
Nothing close to remorse

Speaking truth with no pause
The words of the people will not go ignored
We bringing the force
Revolution
Knocking down doors
Of course
No violence
Cause peace is what I'm fighting for

-ELITE-
4-25-09

In retrospect, the knowledge you possess is
measured by your mental capacity
-ELITE-

THE SECRET

My skin is aching dreams are chasing me
I'm sitting patiently waiting faithfully
For the day my fait is fully awakening
Before the day of reckoning
I'm basically aiming for eternity
Lyrically thru spoken word
I reach the stars beyond infinity
Until then I live my life with tranquility
Life is a trilogy
With three parts
Birth, growth, and death
It's your destiny
Creations getting the best of me
Writing gets the best out of me
Poetry gets the most out of me
While I'm surrounded by lethargy
In a world full of anarchy
I visualize then materialize my thoughts
Revolve synchronize with the sun and gain strength
To go on like krypton's only son
Perform at a level beyond that which will allow me to survive
the storm

-ELITE-

VISINE

Red eyes
Blood shot smoke in the sky
Noticeable high
Grubbin on everything in sight
Full clip wild'n out
Roach tips blunt aroma on your fingerprints
Zoned out enjoying the mood relaxin
With your entourage attractive
The moments an attraction roller coaster malpractice
Forever lasting in another world as it's rolled over
You wake up in present time
You're still sober
The high times is over
Wishing you could go back to when cloud nine was closer

7/08

AMERICA'S NIGHTMARE

The Roswell incident
So secretive
Doesn't exist in the mind of the innocent
Lets just tell'em it was a weather balloon
They'll eat it up with the rest of their pop culture
And *MTV* news
The poison being fed from our eyes thru our ears
Up to our brains
We look the other way
If you saw something, you're insane
So keep your thoughts to yourself
Everything else is contained
Keep your mouths shut
Or forever lose your name
In vain
I choose to fight thru the pain
Latino pride all the way
But I think we all came from Spain
There is a truth and a lie to every story that's told
Like the Egyptians built those pyramids
And their really that old
Or did we go back from the future and colonize the whole
globe?
Extraterrestrials taking over our souls
Controlling our every move with a chip and unfamiliar probes
Masons and their Masonic approach
Secret societies existing in the realms are a joke
2012 as we wait for the illuminati
With their religion, one currency, and one government body
My freedom of speech may end up costing dearly
But I believe what I speak
Listen up close and clearly
We pursue evil missions
And make aggressive decisions
We point the finger at the weak
And shoot to kill never missing
They wake up to busted shots
Like nocturnal emissions

We make out to be the victims
With controlled demolitions
All the lies left and right
I can't help but implode
Instead, I speak out and let my verbal explode
Not knowing in what kind of world my kids are going to grow
Therefore, I'll let my pen do the talking and the pages throw
the blows
Though the color of your skin does nada during conflict
The color of your skin defines you and your conscience
Defines the nonsense
Their concepts change when American wants it to
But the media can't control me or influence my conscious
They wanna' tell you what's real and what's actually fake
Like believing Christ came from heaven and died for our sake
But am I suppose to believe the "king of pop" was disgraced?
Or was he a victim of the same plague
Like the case of a shot rapper with no trace
A set up with no name
I never draw conclusions without knowing the facts
But that's a nightmare to our leaders and their hypocritical acts
With their political rats
Suits and tie racks
About me, they know jack
Our country is under an internal attack
You're chasing dreams but waking up to nightmarish setbacks
Technique said it best on a track
Don't sell your soul to the devil because you'll never get it back
If this was the 50s this poem would be so forbidden
But my thoughts and opinions, I will never keep hidden
They tell you our war was caused and won in Iraq
We really lost
Look at the proof in our troops
Bring'em back!
Now don't get confused with this poem
Not a rap
I get my point across smoothly
Using nothing but facts
So what it rhymes
I put words together carefully
So you can visualize my thought process gracefully

We fight for the same oil they make you pay in gallons for
Then tell us that we need it
Or you can't survive no more
Land of the free
But you have to pay for your freedom
Whether its money or blood
For no particular reason
If you turn back its treason
Telling the truth can be the same as shooting a gun
To say there's no cure for aids
Is to tell me there's no area 51
But knowing too much can also prove to be lethal
Therefore, I'll take in all your lies and make believe we're all
equal
You can believe in fairy tales from within your cerebral
But fact remains the truths always secluded from the people
You can believe in the next man as much as a conspiracy
theorist
My words will never die God
I'll be reciting in spirit
I know I'm a pawn in this war against truth
But if I sell any books, I'll be most thankful to you
Home of the brave
But speak too much and you're thru
Mr. X and King Martin
They were erased too much they knew
All the knowledge they grew
Your bravery will get you so far
Before you are screwed
It's not a direct shot at our democracy of hypocrisy
Just a revelation for those that don't believe in prophecies
I'm on a conspiracy mission

Like what in reality is the true meaning of religion?
If you're stuck in the middle
You're in a very tight position
But you can't allow them to guide you or make your own decisions
It's like a full course collision
I'll choose the latter
Only you yourself decide what in your heart truly matters
Yet it's hard to resist
Diversity doesn't exist
Immortality can't be reached for we are programmed to get sick
Our minds our naïve
Opportunities missed
Controversially written inspired by life
Open your minds but close your eyes and remember think twice
Wake up now and realize this nightmare is precise
Thru the eyes of the blind, I can see the smallest fixture
I tell stories thru my scriptures
If a Polaroid is worth a thousand words
Than this is a motion picture

-ELITE-

THE LAUREATE

The wisdom of King Solomon
Poetry is my temple
Like a poet laureate
Displaying his eminent potential
Being awarded a prize
For his creative mental
Taking the world by storm
Thru his poetical ventures
Studying ancient cultures
Like an archaeologist
Surviving till the end never dying
Like the lead protagonist
Gregariously
Rapidly extracting thoughts from your brain avidly
Extorting your personal views for personal preservation
Artistic gratification
Following the leader of a mosque or church for public
humiliation
My poetry is alienation for the narrow minded
Sensitive souls need not read further
Stop and rewind it
The simple minded are misguided
I'm not here to lead nor mislead
Like John Smith or Columbus leading their troops to greed
Calling it discovery when in reality they're actually thieves
Try'na do right before wrong
Still your God feels forsaken
Going extinct like a Canaanite
Still my words are mistaken
Poetry is a God given gift
Still for granted my words are taken
Prodigal knowledge wasted on sheets
Poetical prowess a prodigy of his own mystique
Like king Arthur's knights of round table
Sir Lancelot with the pen writing fables
During recessions, literature in verse is still stable
Economic downfall like the Berlin wall
Late night cravings satisfied by white castle

Scalpel in hand infiltrating your brain with doubts
Hostile takeover like Bush did the White House
Literary elegance disguised as excellence
Unique approach
Angelic words sensitive thoughts written in superlative
Poet laureate riding his chariot to ceremony
Writing savages middle passages stories of alimony
Describing the struggle surviving the rubble thru the times like matrimony
Materialized mental activity is precious
And to be able to manifest it to life vicarious
It's like the scene of the setting sun
Ocean tide collide aquatic ambience magnified
Poetry at its best
Showcased by the laureate
No remorse no regrets
It only leads to loneliness
No time to regress lets
All learn to express
In harmony with unity for the community
Equals diplomatic immunity
Job security
In this demoralized economy
Officially appointed by a monarchy
Enjoying political freedom like anarchy
Thomas Jefferson expressing his views liberally
A sign of honor
To conquer with ethics and morals
Poetic justice is served with grace as I'm crowned with laurel

-ELITE-

3/11

LOVE AND
ROMANCE

BROKEN HEART

Torn
Split in two half's
Mourn
Blood dripping through its path
Mad
The visualization of a broken hearts wrath
Dullness travels through its veins
Its rate is weak
Its beat's going insane
The heat turns into cold
The warmth becomes chill
Distraught at best
It's like having an ice box in my chest
It shatters as the transformation commence
Sad drips of depressed liquid pouring out the ventricles
The hearts bumping slowly sentimental
Circulation is stopped by the mood no sensations
Going through the brain
Emotional breakdown coming from the main veins
Nerves shake
Tastes buds dissipate
Your soul decapitates
Clogged arteries
No harmony
Intense state
But the beat goes on
Even though the heart breaks

9-18-2009

BELIEVE

I believe
When I think of you it's like my own seed
I believe
Through your eyes I can see the whole galaxy
Extreme supreme feelings of obligation for me
To make sure that you're well taken care of bee
Since your infancy
My sole purpose is to reach thee
Epitome of what a big brother should be
An embodiment of brother sisterly love
Sent from above
I would gladly donate every organ
Just to keep you above
The most beautiful lest thing in this world
I'll serve 1000 jail sentences
Break promises
Repent; commit sins all for the sake of your undying happiness
My best friend
My sibling
My mood ring
My everything
My weakness
My sword when I cut a rug
Strength materialized when I think of you
For you I'll wear my heart on my sleeve
Forever my baby sis
Through you I believe

12-09

-ELITE-

HOPELESS LOVE

Fraudulent acts
Bipolar attacks
Back tracked my love life was trapped
Believe what you will but I know the facts
I'm done with the crap
The two face the snakes and the double-crossing rats
Anger builds up to boiling point
Enough!!!
Then we both blow up like volcanoes erupt
Then insanity struck
I was stuck in a world that I couldn't give up
A love that I couldn't conquer
Sleepless nights intertwined with my thoughts
I'd just ponder and wonder through time and space
About why I was put in this position
I wonder
I starved with all my energy to make it work
I hunger
But our collapse was too much for me to take
Downward spiral to an abysmal pit of disgrace
He said she said resurface on my plate
Lack of trust and understanding's a spit in my face
So as the skies open up and the dark clouds go by
I only think about the good and wont bother to ask why

8/09

-ELITE-

CAN'T MOVE ON

Upside down smile
Sunshine frown
Circumstances make you a killer clown
Your facial features plagued by your facial expressions
Tear drops running down the cheeks
Anger and rage as you're stomping down your feet
It's like cold heat
But happiness is bliss every time you reminisce
The fight's the kiss
Everything in between is hit and miss
All is detailed in my nightly dreams
Waking up everyday with nobody to please
Open eyes look around but no one is seen
The mirror reflects who you used to be
But your true existence hides inside, it's too deep
So as the sun and moon trade places
Everyday brings new and different faces
But in my heart your image remains engraved with all its graces

9-09

-ELITE-

JOURNEY WITH NO PATH

From a distance you captivated my heart
Your spiritual and mental presence was enough to keep me
from falling apart
You were the best friend that I couldn't have
A journey with no path
Emptiness
Like my head with no hat
My souls naked at last
Like my closest relative at a time when no one understood my
past
The internal struggles
Caused by a venomous wrath
When I felt like disappearing you kept me visible
My foolishness has often cost me to lose a friend
But my heart was too lonely to see through the end
I make amends
The realities of circumstances are never apparent
But I am in the right frame of mind state to know better
My conscious is clear
I've weathered the storm but your presence is near
Always kept dear
Now I can't cope with the fact that my hearts in tears
My souls in a secluded atmosphere
And although I am an outcast surrounded by sin
I'll never forget you who allowed me to win
You're the purest angel amongst a pack of demons
You're the rarest form of honesty and reason
You were my voice on the other side of that lifeline
Price tag for you read infinite
The truest form of any light shown from dark
Through the depth in your eyes I can see all my sins
And we knew in our hearts we had done no wrong
But I guess our friendship was way too strong
Your reality sparks my Corazon gets a jump start
Together forever never apart
Maybe in distance but never at heart

2009
-ELITE-

127

LETTER TO THE LOVE OF MY LIFE

To: my precious gem,

I have collected stones and rocks in my life, and in the midst of not realizing what I had, I lost a precious diamond. A priceless ruby red gem that I may never ever find again due to its rarity. I also sold my heart and now I just have an ice box occupying its place...I cant breath, I cant sleep, I cant live without it...Living without this diamond is like kryptonite to my superman... She consumes my every being and now I am broke, poor, and homeless where when I had this priceless piece, I was rich!

To the love of my life

-ELITE-
7/01/08

LOVE MAKING

IN THE HEAT OF THE NIGHT, WHEN FLAMES
IGNITE
Through THE SHEETS THE SPARK FROM THE Light,
GENERATED BY THE ELECTRICITY 2 BODYS
FORM SHINES Bright
UNDER THE COVERS ONLY THE BEDS A WITNESS,
FROM THE DISTANCE, YOU CAN HEAR THE
PASSIONATE CRIES, AS TIME FLYS BY, YOU REACH
CLIMAX TIME,YOU BUST
A TEAR DROPS FROM YOUR EYE, IT WAS MORE
THAN LUST,
THE GRASP OF A PASSIONATE HUG,
RATHER INTENSE AS EVERYTHING MAKES
SENSE, FEELINGS OF WARMTH,SENTIMENT,INTI
MACY,FONDNESS, AND AFFECTION
COULD NOT BE FOUND IN A FLING, U FEEL THAT
SPIRITUAL PRESENCE,
AS YOU ENGAGE IN PHYSICAL CONNECTION,
MIND, BODY, AND SOUL BECOME ONE
IN UNISON, REGARDLESS OF WHAT 2MORROW
MAY POSSESS
FOR THE MOMENT, HEAVENS YOUR ADDRESS,
IN THE MOMENT PEACE IS TEMPORARILY
ETERNAL, AS IT IS INTERNAL
I SPEAK WISDOM,, SOUND ASLEEP
HARMONIZING
FLOWERS FLOURISH BLOSSOMS BLOSSOM
THE TRANQUILITY OF A DOVE
FOR IT WASN'T JUST FUCKING, IT WAS MORE
LIKE MAKING LOVE!
11/04/06
-ELITE-

MOON SHADOW

I use to like how my moon looked at me
How it made my day's dark and my nights bright
How it use to influence my mood
How it would warm me up but keep me cool
I couldn't imagine a world without it
But I got use to living with the sun
I loved its attention and how it made me feel
But the moon
Sometimes it would decide to create clouds over me
It was at its prettiest when it was full
But it would often show itself to me only in half
That's what would cause alarm
The mood would change depending on its orbit
Total eclipse of the sun
Forced me to gravitate towards the opposite direction
Torn between day and night
The moon and the sun
Darkness and light
Happiness or depression
Understanding and confusion
But in the midst of it all
I stayed strong pushed on and attempted do no wrong
Moved forward
My moon couldn't keep rain from falling
I will always look up and see it and know
That my love was true
I just hope you realize it
Because that moon was you

10-2009

-ELITE-

MOVING ON

Tryna' move on
Tryna' stay strong
Tryna' cope with insanity
It's taking too long
But through all the wrong
I am fit to ride through the storm
Taking nothing for granted
And bringing everything along
With my helmet on
Tight singing my same song
I've wiped away tears from my face
I've traveled through space
I've reminisced about the good ole
And even the bad days
Yea I made some mistakes
And i am paying today
But all this misery and pain
Wasn't suppose to be my fait
I don't deserve all the hate
My love is worth more then any disgrace
So I continue to chase
For the heart beat that awaits
But it seems no matter how fast I run
I am always running in place
Even from my dreams I be tryna' escape
Just to wake up and still see your face

10-09

-ELITE-

THANK YOU

When it snowed, you kept me warm
Your mere presence was enough to make the dark clouds
swarm off
As the rain poured, you held an umbrella keeping my dry
You held my hand so that I wouldn't wonder alone in the night
During the emptiest times you opened up the skies, kept me
alive and opened up my eyes
With sincerity, you caught me by surprise
Modesty
In all honesty
It's like lost treasury
You shaded my eyes when the sun was too bright
Never a lie
Your aura made me forget how much I wanted to cry
It is like a river to nowhere
One that ran strait through my heart
You were filtered h2o clear right from the start
Wind breeze blowing purified air
The fear of tears disappear
The tears become clear before they appear
My spirit reappears and swims across the heart filled waters
Dodging lies, insecurities, no time for scrutiny and
Mind-blowing stories erased
Based on your sweet symphony that carelessly whispered into
my soul

As it brought music into my being and joy into my world
When otherwise it was just an abyss like pit of depression
Because of your song and the ocean that ran with it
My heart has been able to heal
Your fountain of youth has nurtured all wounds
I cannot swim, but I am drifting away as the current brings me
to the end of where the river runs dry
You are on the other side standing nearby
A river to nowhere
You throw me a life jacket and get me right out
I see water I see sky I see life
Everything around me is blue
I daze at your person
And simply say thank you

-ELITE-

10-09

TRUE BEAUTY

I get lost in your visual
Fixated by your look, but your beauty's just material
I'm looking for something deeper, original, spiritual, and
mental
Until I learn your interior
I'll settle for staring at your physical
However I need something more then just exterior
But damn your stunning sex appeal has me tapping my heals
Your elegance and grace has my mind running in place
Wondering through space as I admire your face
But I reiterate that I need more than just something to lace
I want to invade your space, get into your brain, infiltrate you
mind state
Then make a hefty escape into your heart
Captivate your soul and generate a spark
Get to know the inner you and make cupid shoot you with
darts
I want to get trapped in your eyes and see a thousand skies
See the world, universe, and galaxy as we fly
Read between the lines and experience your life
Smell the heavenly flowers as I gaze at your smile
Internal beauty is more my style
Your outsides are impressive but your insides I desire
So show me your true beauty and light a match under this fire

12-09

-ELITE-

MADRE MIA

Me estuviste en el vientre
9 meses
8 libras de amor eres fuerte
En el presente
Hoy vivo pendiente
Y reconosco todas las luchas para poder criarnos
Quidarnos
Aun trabajando
Para despues llegar a limpiar y a cocinarnos
Estoy tratando
De expresarme
Literalmente liricamente
Con lectura
Echando mi Corazon en la pagina para dejarte
Saber que te quiero
No tienes que leerlo
Pero se que no lo enseño
Pero en el enquentro
Esta es mi manera de decirlo
Quisiera tenerte toda mi vida
Todos los dias
I love you mom para siempre
Madre mia

-Jeff-

9-14-10

YOUR LIPS

Your lips match your eyes
Which I can see inside
Stare you down from your hips to your thighs
Strip search you from behind
But a glance never lies
It goes well with your vibe
Your hair your smile
They all attract but nothing compares
They all connect but nothing is as carefully cared
As those lips
That lip gloss ya, wearing
Makes me want to hip toss ya, I'm staring
It's like juices flowing
My pupils growing
Just gazing at what appears to be flavorful fruits of passion and
love
Moist tenderness I just can't get enough of...
Those lips
I'm in a trance when I reflect on how they use to feel pressed up
against mine
All types of feelings and emotions running down the spine
Those lips
The fine-tuned texture
Reveals and highlights your true glow
It's the single most articulate artery, vein, and nerve that I'm
addicted to the most on you
Erogenous for intimacy
The blood circulates as I navigate my way through the borders
And volcanic groove of your pucker uppers
Every perfect line creates just enough attraction
To make me want to
Come closer and kiss you
I'm addicted to
Your lips

-ELITE-

2-09

TEN TWENTY ONE TEN

The pact was made months in advance
That we would meet up at the park and start a romance

Anxiety attacked me as the day dragged by
I couldn't wait until 6pm to reunite with my future bride
A million thoughts crossed my mine
As the time approached
Will she show or will she ditch
Or will my foolishness combined with pride
Be a bitch

The pact was made about 6 months in advance
That we would meet up at the park
And start our romance

I had a fresh cut,
Shit I was looking type sharp
Although it seemed very cheesy
I was convinced it was smart
To meet up at the park where we spent countless days before

Feeding birds
Walking dogs
Jogging
Lovebirds intertwined with nature
Enjoying each others company
This point of interest was our land mind
Focal point properly
Significantly we

Made a pact in advance
That we would meet up here
On your birthday and commence
Our eternal romance

Although we had grown apart
The pact still stood

And if we both showed up
We would be together for good

I had not made a decision
Couldn't make up my mind
But I wasn't fooling anyone
Had to put my pride aside
I tried telling myself that I wasn't sure
But we all knew I would be there and square
After all, I wouldn't dare
Stand up the girl that had always been there
Who had been through it all with me for years
Who saw me break hearts
And receive the same equally
Through thick and thin
Together peacefully
She who would have my child and raise him successfully
Who would wife my house with a smile

I had it all planned
I would arrive with flowers in hand
And a gift in its box
I was thinking out of the box
Like a jack in a box
Sweat and fear condensated my car
Waiting patiently for my future
Watching the rest of my life from afar
But there was nothing to fear
Because

We had made a pact
Way back in advance
That we would meet up at the park
And begin our romance

Then my biggest fear began to materialize
The clock was my doom
And nobody in sight
The hours came and went
Judgment day symbolized
As I held back tears
I've never wanted to cry

But as darkness took over
Reality struck very slow
But the "love of my life"
Never decided to show
Therefore, I drove off
Drowning in my own pool
With no manhood and dead flowers
Happiness left no room
Like a rotten corpse
Driving away to his tomb

But why?
When the pact had been made
So long in advance
Where we would meet at Passaic Park
And begin our romance

-ELITE-

11/10

WITHOUT YOU

My nights are endless journeys thru darkness
An abyss of eternal damnation
A gutless pit of hell
Sleep is nothing but a mere afterthought
A craving no less
Cries for help are silenced by fear
Terror takes away sound before I make one
I'm doomed
Without you
There's no meaning
Definition has no definition
I'm secluded
Trapped in an abysmal chamber of misery
The thought of loneliness fills my heart
With sorrow
It pumps sadness into my blood
And pain into my veins
Like a baster squirting juice on a turkey
It's like no water when I'm thirsty
In a dessert only mirages
My mind bursts in temptation is lurking
But depression consumes my being
It limits me
Takes its toll
Ages me
I become irrelevant, non-existent, extinct
Without you
I'm nothing

-JEFF-

11-21-08

NO COMPARISON

I compare you to that lifeline that I never want to use
Just knowing that you are there is satisfying
Gratifying
But its you
Therefore, I'm at peace

I compare you to that risk that I never want to take
Scared of failure and getting hurt
But I seek the thrill so I escape
But its you
Therefore, I'm free

I compare you to that friend who I never want to let go
Afraid to be without you but I just dangle you on a rope
But I give you enough air
Therefore, you will never choke
And you are still you
Therefore, I feel at ease

I'm trying to compare you but I really cannot
Therefore, I'll just embrace you
And let the comparing stop
You are the light at the end of the tunnel
Peace
Freedom
Mental ease
Tranquility
And your still you so I'm serene

-ELITE-

9-2-10

STORYTELLERS

They are so because they tell stories
When I look at them, your life flashes by mine
They remind me of the skies, and how its aquatic colors define
life
They incorporate nature when its green represents grass and
symbolizes the earth
They tell stories when I stare at them
They remind me of how life is short and deserves to be
cherished
They describe a nice walk in the park on a sunny day
I cannot help but gaze into them and lose myself in a maze
In merely seconds time elapses like days
They are what I crave
War becomes peace at a glimpse of them
They transform chaos to tranquility
Like a symphony
They will turn your worst mood serene
Thru them, I see the heavens
Hell does not exist with a sight so pure
Stunning visual as I visualize
What I see I'm dumb mesmerized
They tell no lies as they foretell lives
They reflect like a mirror
Shine like a star
They are like translucent lights
Thru them I can fly
You can see the whole world
They are your eyes
They are storytellers

-ELITE-

2008

IDYLLIC ATTRACTION

You were *geekin,*
Tight stretch jeans
Cell was *beepin*
Along came 'Elite'
Had you *speakin*
The *freakin*
The attraction was the different mind state
Wanted to discover your buried treasure
Like Benjamin Gates
Nationally
Wanted to make love to you carelessly
Passionately
Ideal piece correct
Rugged and raw
Sexy persuasive
I could take you to war
Philosophical
The way you navigate thru my mind
Hair down
Astronomical and aerodynamic
Lip-gloss glistening
Nothing extravagant
Compliment me in any ambience
Lady like
But elegantly gangsterish
Knows about the life of the impoverished
Hungry
Ghetto queen
My main squeeze
Never my girl but always my fav boo
We use to joke about the best orgasm I ever gave you
My damsel in distress
In high heels
Mass appeal
Self-respect
Stress
Worth of self
Immorality means you're just another notch under a belt

But you put the real in *k.i.r.a*
In this social decadence
We thrive together
Deprivation of depravity doesn't exist
But you make me wanna believe decency's your gift
Always on point
Thick
Ride or die chick
Slick
In the gutter but rich
Certain jaggedness
Wearing hoodie fatigues
But in a ballroom looks glamorous
Who knows how to switch
Athletic quite nice
You're on my mind
But thru a rhyme, this sheet brought you to life

-ELITE-

3/10

YOUR VOICE NEXT TO MINE

We traveled thru time
Thru each others minds
For 2 hours
Exhausting the phone lines
Attention span surrendered
Eardrums serenaded
Smooth sounds of your vocal cords
Making my sleep depredated
The knowledge exposed
Had my mentals deliberating
Salivating
Contemplating a future
As Verizon satellites were hesitating
Service interrupted
But the interest wasn't corrupted
The thought process grew with mass appeal
3am displayed on the clock
Your voice was real
Rest was far-fetched
But I could care less
For at the moment
I only wanted to hear the sweet
Sound of your breath
As you said…"goodnight"
And into the sunset

-ELITE-

7-19-10

EVOLUTION OF US

On a bench he sat at the palisades mall
Waiting for love down from heaven to fall
Patiently waiting as shoes kept passing by
Waiting for that face that he would finally recognize
Little did he know that his day would soon get bright
For that smile on her face could light up the night
With a gentle hug they embraced
Her tender lips would drift him away to a serene place
She had the criteria of a future wife
The one you bring home to mom and learn to satisfy life
He could spend the whole day with her just collaborating
Doing nothing at all, she's an adventure worth dating
Silky smooth sazon vanilla Goya
Both her beauties are enough to paranoia
Inner and outer
Dominican love
He gets lost in her eyes
He sees hearts from above
Traditionally
He gets a sense of freedom
Sexually
There's no need for reason
Two scorpions stinging each other with their presence
The poison reached both their hearts in a second
The mind sent a message
Cupid walked away smiling
Knowing that they had learned a lesson
Chemistry is born that which cannot be destroyed
No matter what occurs their bond will never show void
As long as they have each other, they'll always have joy
The passions secure
It all started in a chat room
Now the minds are one
Pure
The evolution of two hearts
Couldn't be more obscure

-ELITE-
3/10

146

TIC TAC TOE

We cross paths everyday
We are in this closed box with no way to escape
When I come, you go
When you come, I go
It's like a big giant game of tic tac toe
A line goes through us
With a space in between
An O occupies that vacancy
As we X out our feelings
3 in a row has no meaning
It's not a game
Mental breakdown has nothing to do with the brain
Therefore, you stay in your corner
I will stay in mine
Xs and Os describe our love at one time

-ELITE-

6-21-10

ROMANTIC ESCAPE

Rose pedals guiding your path
Silk sheets warm water in the bubble bath
Feeling the heat
Scented candles illuminate the room
Setting the mood
Sexual tension marks the start
Milk chocolate kisses on the bed forming a heart
Bubbly on ice
Relaxations the feeling tonight
The realization of a love worth the fight
Sensuality surrounding the scene
Seafood
The hot sauce may be used for foreplay later
The nocturnal passionate cries will surely disturb the neighbors
The pleasurable things in life deserve to be cherished
Romance
Coming from the core of a ghetto Romeo
Swagger on point from the barrio
Sexual
Caressing every curve in your body
Like it's natural
Whip cream
Going half on a seed
But using a magnum as collateral
Sunsets
The quiet symphony of two resting breaths
Serenity feels correct
Sensuality with nothing but elegance and grace
Allow me to take you away on a romantic escape

-ELITE-

4-26-10

WONDERING

She was the rib from my cage
Well rounded
Same age
Never realized it then
But she was a coming of age
Gold mine that slipped through my grasp
Never take for granted the possessions you have
Ashamed and spent
I'm thinking back at what came and went
Something special deserves to be cherished
Acknowledge it early before it is perished
In a commitment the one who gives all
Usually has all the leverage
So now, I kick back with an alcoholic beverage
Sit back and think of how it could have ended up in marriage
No luck when this love games a savage
It does damage
Now my minds on a rampage
Wondering if I'll ever find love again

-ELITE-

Revised from 3/08

DARKNESS

TRAGEDIES

Ever since the fall of the twins
Shits never been the same
Evil begins
Lurking through the walls taking over with sin
Years of dark clouds hovering over us
Plus the hate is merely a crust
Of the pure black cats crawling within the dust
Trust
Beelzebub is at peace when the world is in heat
We must cool it off so more people can eat
Learn from defeat
Unify so maybe more heads can have a permanent seat
And maybe more can achieve
Instead of thinking give we think receive
But that's one of the worlds most fucked up tragedies
Wars, rumbles, casualties
We fight over pettiness
Nobody stops to get their minds right
Silliness
We can all be royal
We're mostly in loyal
Instead we scuffle for what another man has
If not for oil
We're cursed with a brain that can take over destroy you
We invent ways to kill ourselves
If not they do it for you
2 ways to be raised
Disciplined and spoiled
Man made computer chips can extinct us into the soil
We in one world
But we fight for blocks and nationalities like
That street you hug doesn't hug you back right
Welfare lines stacked regardless of rain
When the skies are dry the sunshine's polluted
No fish to fry unless you have pie
Unemployment rates at all time highs
Consequences

Every action has a reaction
And it comes with a price
We cannot control hurricanes or earthquakes
Tornadoes or when our world shakes
But for the most part
We control our fates
They say a mind is a terrible thing to waste
Unfortunately for our youth
With all the negativity inflicted upon them
They're left with no choice
Nothing positive for them to follow
So they listen to the devilish voice
No strategy
And in today's society
That's by far the biggest tragedy

-ELITE-

LONELINESS

Loneliness motivates me to get to know myself
To dig deep down inside and get to grow with myself
To form literary wealth
To captivate my soul and prolong its health
Loneliness gives me the courage I need to triumph
It keeps me humbled and grounded
I can feel the serenity no matter how loud the noise sounded
I can hear tranquility within my thoughts
Loneliness forces you to get in touch with you inner being
Causes you to learn your inner most intimate desires, fears, and goals
It gives you endless time to sort our priorities
It allows you to determine who's important and who's not
Who's real and who's not
What's cold and what's hot
When it strikes you'll know the times right
For you to reflect, analyze, and vent with self
So when loneliness attacks
Learn how to keep yourself company
Mind, body, and soul in harmony
Cause at the end of the day you come and go alone
Trust this

-ELITE-

2-2010

TORN

God my heart is torn between the loves that you have blessed upon me.

Instead of joy and happiness, it only brings more stress upon me.

The only thing I tried to do was to better her life,
And take her dark and gloomy world and try to bring forth more light.
And make it bright.

She has opportunity and potential of becoming my wife,
But she is blinded by her emotion; he doesn't even treat her right.
But yet and still I'm the one she's trying to kick out of her life,

And stay in a relationship that sounds like Tina and Ike's.
What do I do to make her see that I will never give up?
It's a promise and guarantee that I'll always live up.

Lord please help me rid her of her insecurities,
They're probably a side effect from always burning dem' trees.

I cannot force her to have faith, I cannot tell her what to think.
You can lead a horse to water, but you can never make it drink.

It's a lesson taught from life that she'll have to learn on her own.
I learned the lesson myself and, Lord, now look how I've grown.

However, I don't want her to go thru such an extreme lesson.
Cause it'll put you thru a world of stress, unrest, and depression.

She has already been thru enough; she doesn't need extra stressin',
Because I'm afraid, she'll end up going in the wrong direction.
   I don't want her falling victim to the belly of the beast,
And get caught up in its clenches and get grinded in its teeth.
   She needs to know there's more to life than what's out here in these streets.
Money can't buy you love, happiness, or internal peace.
   Therefore, I keep it discrete, but I refuse to let her share the fate of so many others.
Unstable yet, she doesn't need to be another mother.
   What will it take her to realize I am not going anywhere?
If she calls on you or me, she knows we'll always be there.
   I know that in the past it was hard for her to find people to trust.
But what I bear for her is unconditional love, it's not lust.
   I done tried everything in my power, now its all in your hands.
I will always do all that I can, but I am only one man.
                    Amen.

-ELITE-

???????

LOCAL ABADDON

I walked past a fiery lake
Approached a pool of blood
Disaster everywhere
Constant floods
Emotional apocalypse
Arrived at the gates
Pits of hate
Nothing but dark entities await
It closes shut as the chains are locked
My souls stuck
An evil figure shows up
Introduces himself with multiple names
But all I see is a shadow
I thought it was death
Walking negativity
Flames shooting out of his breath
He held a mirror in front of me
Even my thoughts would reflect
It started getting very hot as I started to sweat
Showed accounts of my whole life
Starting from birth
Beginning with pain, it ended with a curse
No sense of remorse his stare could cause thirst
Suddenly blinded by a sharp light
I realized it was hell on earth

-ELITE-

2/10

WHY

At only 52, you were taken from us. The nicotine and booze
took its toll. You did not even get a third strike

Just a 2nd swing and a miss and you were out.
Irrational thoughts unraveling and travelling through my head,
as your body fought, but not in vane, your body lost.

A learning experience for all as we fight to maintain,
there is no escaping the train, it is our fait, death.
It comes in all shapes and sizes, never reversing the hands of
time

Although gone, you will forever remain in my mind.
A life is to never be taken for granted.
Nothing can solidify a broken soul, travelling through a broken
sky, so I cry these broken tears from my shattered eyes.

I was your favorite and I did not know why.
I will keep your memory enhanced travelling with my times.

Although you made your mistakes, your life was not worth it,
did not have much, but you gave what you had.
I take a lesson with me, cherish what you have.

I know you are listening right now, so I will say my last
goodbye, emotional I stand, just wondering why...

-ELITE-

R.I.P TIO

MENTAL PURGATORY

I am serving life sentences
In this hell
Sloppy penmanship
Rusty sword mental jail
When my pen is sick
Slaying souls with the *"finish him!"*
Your hearts in my hand
Your blood is thick
I am sending dosages of tranquilizers
That travel thru your system
Reducing frequencies like equalizers
Intertwined
In this game of imprisonment
My written nine
Is my guardian through tough times
I speak my mind
Eloquently when the words shine
On frontlines
Mental collapse is the main crime
Homicide
I match the profile
Elegant
With words of wisdom, in conflicts
I circumvent
Just grab a pen

Spoken thoughts expressed epically
Lyrically
Spoken word is the epitome
I am incarcerated in my surroundings
My mind holds the key to the cellblock confinement
I am drowning
In a pool of alcohol
Depression consumes my being
After all
The tensions my nourishment
Dissecting my enigma
26 years of creativity unleashed
My person comes alive
As he bursts out thru the sheet
Verbal warfare
Cerebral purgatory
As I pronounce my release through my escape
Literature is my camouflage fatigues
Major league combat
Losing is my antifreeze
I play for keeps

-ELITE-

3/10

KNOWLEDGE GOD (17)

To Grandma

One seven
I'll see you in heaven
You were grandma to 17
Mother to nine
Great grand to some
A chill up the spine
The sum of all things
I cannot breath
Tears down my cheeks
I need morphine
I can't sleep
My productivity is weak
We're all headed that route
Now I don't want to dream
You gave me my name
Now you're no longer on the scene
In my mind you are seen
You're in a better heavenly place
Your spirit, your energy
Stays forever engraved
We'll see you in the new system
The paradise
Until then we miss you
Your soft rice
Your tenderness
You're Gods knowledge acknowledged
You died on the 17th
That's knowledge God

-ELITE-

02-09-09

LETTER TO THE UNBORN

Dear my child
I should've been your father
But today I'm just Jeff
I should've had more honor
Instead, I chose your death
All before you ever took your first breath

I didn't practice self-control
Let alone birth control
My "mistake" cost me $500
However, priceless was your soul

I didn't want you growing up
In a life with no home
I didn't want you being born to
A pops who wasn't grown
I had no backbone
But I'd still loved you
I'm sorry

The reason for your prevention
Was somewhat a misconception
More like knowledge deprivation
But I didn't want to father a child
To a girl whom I had no intentions

At my age
Mental state
Current stage in life
I often think of procreation
But at the time
It was nowhere near
My cerebral station

I had a 94' ford
Escort with four doors
But no core and no cure
Miles galore

The ransom to pay for your departure
Was my capital
I was "broke" literally, figuratively, and even spiritually
Torn
May I have done the right thing?
Or was I ready to mourn

I didn't know where to hide
I wanted a certain life for you
That I couldn't provide

I wasn't ready to step up
And for that I apologize
A man of his word
Should always man up to his lies

I wanted you to have both your parents
For that, I take pride
But I used my organs not my heart
To ultimately make up my mind
What a way to decide

These excuses are mine
Yes, I know and understand
It's a shame what had to be lost
All due to a one night stand

An occasional romance
That leads to the occasional casual sexual encounter
It's never planned
But it's too late to go back and make the right corrections
That's the life and times of an adolescent

I always wondered if you would've had my face
Or would you have had a swagger,
Intellect, elegance, grace
Guess I'll never know now

I didn't put you thru the struggle
Although my soul wasn't at peace
I took away your first teardrop
Without you ever meeting me

My promise is to give you brothers and sisters
They won't suffer the same fait
I just hope you can forgive me and my juvenile mistake
As you watch down on me from a heavenly place

-ELITE-

7-23-10

IF I DIE TONIGHT

If I die tonight
I want you to know that I loved you
That no matter what, my heart can't escape how it feels
Although I wasn't "in love" with you
My deep feelings were sincere and real
If I die tonight
I'll go out wearing a Yankee fitted
Survived by my writings
My life is encrypted
Gifted
I'll probably be twisted
Hung-over
Or even lifted
At the end of the day, I will still be me
Prolific
I'll die with a cold heart
Flame extinguished
Donate my organs for a good cause
Positive ending
Instinctive
No drama
I will go peacefully
Knowing that the worlds pain didn't drive me
To delinquency
Just know that I'll definitely say bye before I go
Deliberately
And if I didn't it means, I'll still be here tomorrow

-ELITE-

3/10

INCARCERATED SOULS

Incarcerated souls
Roaming this world with ho home
No hope
Trapped in a black hole
With no growth
The sunlight is obstructed by smoke
Potential knowledge is diluted
With hazardous garbage
Harmful contaminants
Deteriorating our physical mind states
Hate is the wasted energy
That's overtaken and overwhelmed our society
The crime rate
At an all time great
The soul struggles
Spirit hustles
But can't cope
There's no hope
Negativity has its own way of killing slow
So stay positive

-ELITE-

2/10

UNTITLED

Extreme sadness as I have a tsunami wave coming right at me
A wave filled with anger, stress, and depression
As I just stand there with my eyes closed and hope that I will
be safe
From these emotions in motion.
As I take my last breath and dive, I open my eyes and find
myself
Bombarded with life
In the midst of everything, no one sees my cries for help as I'm
drowning
I may have my life held together by duck tape but inside I'm
filling up with water
And as I feel the weight on my shoulders pushing me down
The image of what makes me happy drew upon my vision and I
let myself go
Cuz' I don't want to keep fighting for air
-From yube-

-ELITE-

05-26-10

EPILOGUE

LETTER FROM THE DEAD

To Whom It May Concern:
Although I'm gone, my spirit lives on
My body's no more, but my mind is still strong

Being on earth was merely an experience
A part of life, a journey, which we take much too serious
The path neither starts nor ends in the material form
The physical being just makes the spiritual born
I was given this opportunity to write to those who care
Those interested will read this and realize I'm still there

I will not give too much away
For father will be angry
Just know your existence is forever
Even if you don't understand me
There are things that go on thru time and space
That even I cannot see

I have been watching from above
And wondering why
The physical worlds full of hate
Making us cry

I have been advised to warn you
Of the devilish wrath
For Satan will bite you
Unless you choose a righteous path
So beware, but never fear
Because we're watching down
You cannot control everything
Not even your own outcomes now

Therefore, you have to stay focused
On what's important in life
Because gifts come to those
Who've been not naughty but nice

Your stay on earth is temporary
Your permanent home is here with us
We will await your return
As soon as Father says, it is just

Just know we will be waiting with opened arms
Just reach for the sun
Trust you will know it is us
Whenever your time comes

P.S
Love conquers all, even if hatred strikes first
Weather the storm, as it will only get worse

Love you
-Unknown-

7-7-7th of eternity

OUTRO

Driving towards the abyss
With no rearview mirrors
No brakes just gas
Speeding pass the past
Greener pastures is the path
But you reach eternal damnation
Alas!

4/10

CONCLUSION

Conclusion is the ending of a composition in the form of a coda
or outro
Time to outgrow
The child inside who allows the journey to unfold
Gun ho
Excitement unravels as the powder from the verbal gun blows
Like a snub-nosed
Extinction of the dinos
As the story unfolds
Meteor shower on the page as it kills all words
Using proverbs
This book was an English lesson to those who observed
Apocalypses' revelations all predicting demise
But only time will tell if the end will ever materialize

THE GRAND FINALE

The final thoughts of an Egyptian pharaoh
A martyr
Where the mind set's never narrow
Sharp like an arrow
But humbled
Never shallow
Now the last pieces of the puzzle come together
Alive
Taking its last breath
Stay awake for sleep is just a cousin of death
Casual
Reserved conservative
Unique style preservative
This is the closing credits, conclusion
Equivalent to an Amen
From the aliens back to the cavemen
Of mice and made men
Describing the life of myself through the words and eyes of the
stealth
Wise words are felt
This is my closing argument as we reach a verdict
From afar it looks vague but in your face it is perfect
Golden child
Like a chosen kid
Promiscuous
But there's a time and place for every action regardless
whether it's positive or negative
Ancient philosopher
Mentality is sometimes questionable
Uninhabitable

But always honest to self
Flawful
With no physical disfigurements, but always learning from
prior mistakes as well as accomplishments
Pour a little liquor on the pavement to clean out the wounds
Symbolize the blood of our ancestors relaxing in their tombs
This is survival
Soon
The end awaits
Doom
You only take with you whatever you knew
Unlocking taboos
Tribal tattoos
Seeking all truth
To the counter productive lets, counter react
 Grown and sexy infantile minds don't know how to act
I'm just ending this thesaurus with some lyrical facts
Just stand strong no need to walk with a clutch
Living in the land of the free is costing too much
This is an ending and a new beginning
Its majesty
Superlative imperative narrative
A grand summary
Nothing less then a prerogative
Opposite of creative travesty
Defining gravity
An Outro
Submerged thoughts summarizing knowledge exposed
A bright Light shining its glow
Intoxication of a New Jersey flow
27 years of life unfold
El fin

Lyrics that the street thirsts for
Supreme
Ambience is serene
Internally creative kingdom bestowing a thrown
Protector
Preeminent writings
 The pen's my scepter
A royal staff to jot down imperial wisdom
Like a baton or magic wand
The powers endowed
Spirit fighting the natural forces of evil colliding
Outlasting time
Finishing with a cosmic boom like Ryu
Friction sparking energy through life forms in rhyme form
Metaphors morph and make your mind transform
Before your eyes
Navigate through time as you realize you're reading a
legendary design
Never compromise
Turn the skeptic into a believer
The most serious of doubters into a series of followers
You're allowed to hurt
Follow the hearse
As the casket closes on a victim
The book closes the chapters combined to form a system
Comprised wisdom
It's an enigma
Feeling of brand new
Divine mathematics
The twelve jewels
Knowledge, wisdom, understanding
Useful tools

Olympian Gods and titans like Greek mythology
Learn to treat your anxieties
Like secret societies
The skull and crossbones
These words inflict cerebral lobotomy
Microsoft word casualties
Virtual reality
It's all apart of me
Cosmic entities of abnormal normality's
Practice morality but its all a technicality
The death of sanity
The birth of technology
Scriptural homicide
Calamity
My words reach and touch the depth of humanity
Often late, I procrastinate but I'm the protagonist
Procreate when the time calls for it
I plant the seeds that'll one day make the planet rotate
I'm leaving my guts all splattered on the sheet
Blood sweat and tears
I'm even spilling my soul out for you to read
This is heat
Sweet street taste of concrete
Anger unleashed
Years of oppressed feelings trapped inside a leash
Like knowing that on my mom my pops cheats
Ages of denial is trivial
I speak in terms of imperial
Mental terrorist but in actuality never a criminal
I'm never senile but its time to redial
And let out these flames I'm being critical
Cynical

All the pain inside me let out through my ventricles
Crucial
6'1 frame but you don't have to look up to see me though
I have special love for those that can read me outside of the
box and find the real me material
Crispy like cereal
Fresh to death standing out at my pinnacle
Don't misinterpret my confidence with cockiness
Outlandish
Don't mistake my lyrical content for mythical nonsense
Nothing malicious in my concepts
Never misinterpretate fait with miracle
It either is or it's not meant
You can't be suicidal and still be alive
Sometimes you have to swallow your ego before you swallow
your pride
Everything has a meaning than you finally die
Never apologize for saying how you feel
That's like me saying sorry for KEEPING IT REAL!
-ELITE-

9-13-10

ADDRESS TO GOD

Let us pray

Jehovah
I come to you head bowed and humbled
To give thanks for everyday I survive in this struggle
To repent for every time that I stumble
Although your kids suffer, I pray and believe there is light at
the end of the tunnel
Until then we will continue to search for you as we look thru
this funnel
I pray for the strength that it takes to get by
As I pray for each day that's gone by
All the while, you look down from the sky
I ask for forgiveness for I know I have sinned
But rest assured I have tried to learn from them as I turn a loss
into a win
And I always try my damnedest to not make the same mistakes
twice
Knowing that Satan is persuasive, he makes the ugly look nice
And so I beg for your forgiveness, I'll try to make all things
right
I express remorse for falling victim to the serpent
And try to lead a righteous path and learn to serve a purpose
I have read the scriptures and the stories your son told
Many a lesson I've learned
Many a cross has been burned
You know thru my writing is how I show what's in my soul
Knowledge that I will forever hold
Therefore, I ask that you guide me so that I can help others in
need
And when it's dark be the light that illuminates the path in
front of me
When I am blind let me see
Open my eyes whenever in need
I say please
I know my mouth has been dirty
Cleanse it out with your grace
Allow me to be positive as I continue this chase

To someday be amongst you in a heavenly place
Thanks for giving me the privilege of having a voice
May it incorporate peace and the ability to rejoice
Allow me to recognize the truth but internally be my own boss
May the memories of those rest in peace that we've lost
I hope I'm not asking too much
I have never been one to glut
For what I need the most is comfort and peace that's the truth
Although I've never expressed myself like this before you know, it's coming from the heart
Sorry for anybody that I've managed to hurt
Let this prayer be the spark of a new start
May the will of the good overthrow that of evil
And let my poems and my words be the voice of the people
I know I have not always believed in you let alone obeyed you
I just never liked the concept of letting others persuade you
That's why I draw my own conclusions and worship within myself
Religion is a concept that I just haven't quite felt
If I am wrong, forgive me for I do not know any better
Just know you are on my mind with every endeavor
You have blessed me with writing as my gift
And if you really do exist
And acknowledge this message
Have mercy on my soul but please spare me the lectures
For I done seen to many things father your children need you!
You have wiped my tears when I've cried but still I can't always please you
The laws are far too difficult to obey but please allow me to ease thru
Allow my imperfections to live thru you
Knowing that in my mind, I want to serve you
But I just swerve thru with no clue hopeless
Therefore, I write down my thoughts in hopes to express views
I'm saying thank you for everything and asking for amnesty
Knowing I don't deserve everything but still trying to be exemplary
I cherish life and take nothing for granted
Straighten me up when my direction is slanted
Just give me vision as I fight thru this mission
I will try to stay grounded during the successes and failures

Bless my pen and the knowledge it leaks
Let these pages be a manifestation of what you and your son speak
But never let me compromise my style as I preach
Keeping my swagger, grace, and intellect unique
I need the power to part red seas like Moses
Thru my words, I will inherit the force of explosives
I need you to instill instincts ferocious
In order to cope with the everyday devils lurkin'
Open my eyes wide to their deception and lies
Allow me to use my words for good and steer positive into lives
Till the day that I die
I give thanks for all the food that I've tasted
Pardon me for all the food that I've wasted
I am grateful for all the spiritual and physical elements that you have blessed me with
I also pray for those that are less fortunate
I pray for my family and ask for their protection
Forever guide us and lead us in the right direction
Allow me to forgive those who have hurt me the way you forgive those who forsake you
Thru my positivity, you turn a grey sky blue
Presence of mind was bestowed
So don't use it against us as we already pay what we owe
I truly believe my decisions are based on the mentality and choices thee has given me
But please lord forgive me for thinking that way for these are the circumstances you've provided me
Our Father, Who art in heaven
Hallowed be Thy Name
Thy kingdom come,
Thy will be done,
on earth as it is in heaven till time lasts indefinitely
Now if my words reach infinity I hope you lead the way
But if not lord let them live for eternity and never ever stray
To you I pray
In Jesus name
Amen
Amen

-ELITE-

ACKNOWLEDGEMENTS

To those who attributed, influenced, inspired, contributed, and/or lent their thoughts, hearts, and/or voiced their opinions as well as ideas in the making of this book and the contents within.
Those who shared their guidance, knowledge and support throughout this process and helped make this project possible. I thank you and acknowledge you:

In no particular order,
Mom and Dad for being the co-creators and procreators
Tasha my baby sis and my backbone
Jose my best friend since the 6th grade
Yube (the official), Jen, Rebecca, "L", Kay, Kat, Abuelitas, Tio Chao, Fern, Mayra, Danny, Eric, Rene, Jonathan, "Steven Jones", "YaYi", "Minnie Mouse", Kattie, Keri Marie, "Justin Time", "Traviiesa", Melanie, Dana, Kelly, Kathy M., Gina G, "Wild Creature", Crystal G., Prima Denisse, Luis, "Poncho", Cammie, Nicole D., Jennifer Diaz, Mirela, Robyn, Podesta (for your artwork), Vee, Enablx, all DeLaRosas, all Robleses, hip-hop, poetry lovers, all other friends, relatives, lost ones, loved ones, higher powers, and everything and everybody relevant

Everybody listed above were used in some capacity, way, shape, or form as motivation, inspiration, guidance, as a focal point, strength, and/or courage in order to complete the mission that is my book. You have all given me inclusive and exclusive ideas, thoughts, memories, and opinions. Whether big or small, you have all made contributions and you have all taken the journey with me consciously and/or subconsciously even if you did not notice or realize it. Your presence, spirit, character, influences, and past participations as well as experiences in the life and times of "ELITE" have touched and grazed these pages. You're names are now and will forever remain immortalized within me.
For those who are not mentioned and feel that they should have been, I am sorry.

Keepin It Real, Always
-JEFF-